Assam Politics in Post-Congress Era

Assam Politics in Post-Congress Era

1985 and Beyond

Sandhya Goswami

SAGE Series on Politics in Indian States
Volume 4

Series Editors
Suhas Palshikar
Rajeshwari Deshpande

Los Angeles I London I New Delhi
Singapore I Washington DC I Melbourne

First published in 2020 by

SAGE Publications India Pvt Ltd
B1/I-1 Mohan Cooperative Industrial Area
Mathura Road, New Delhi 110 044, India
www.sagepub.in

SAGE Publications Inc
2455 Teller Road
Thousand Oaks, California 91320, USA

SAGE Publications Ltd
1 Oliver's Yard, 55 City Road
London EC1Y 1SP, United Kingdom

SAGE Publications Asia-Pacific Pte Ltd
18 Cross Street #10-10/11/12
China Square Central
Singapore 048423

Published by Vivek Mehra for SAGE Publications India Pvt Ltd. Typeset in 10.5/13 pt Berkeley by Zaza Eunice, Hosur, Tamil Nadu, India.

Library of Congress Cataloging-in-Publication Data

Names: Goswami, Sandhya, author.
Title: Assam politics in post-Congress era: 1985 and beyond/Sandhya
 Goswami.
Description: New Delhi, India; Thousand Oaks, California: SAGE, 2020. |
 Series: Series on politics in Indian states | Includes bibliographical
 references and index.
Identifiers: LCCN 2020016171 | ISBN 9789353883645 (hardback) | ISBN
 9789353883652 (epub) | ISBN 9789353883669 (ebook)
Subjects: LCSH: Political parties—India—Assam. | Asama Gana Parishada. |
 Bharatiya Janata Party. | Party affiliation—India—Assam. | Assam
 (India)—Politics and government—20th century. | Assam
 (India)—Politics and government—21st century.
Classification: LCC JQ339.A45 G67 2020 | DDC 320.954/162—dc23
LC record available at https://lccn.loc.gov/2020016171

ISBN: 978-93-5388-364-5 (HB)

SAGE Team: Abhijit Baroi and Satvinder Kaur

To
my father,
the late Rajendranath Barua,
who has been a source of inspiration
throughout my life.

Thank you for choosing a SAGE product!
If you have any comment, observation or feedback,
I would like to personally hear from you.

Please write to me at **contactceo@sagepub.in**

Vivek Mehra, Managing Director and CEO, SAGE India.

Bulk Sales

SAGE India offers special discounts
for purchase of books in bulk.
We also make available special imprints
and excerpts from our books on demand.

For orders and enquiries, write to us at

Marketing Department
SAGE Publications India Pvt Ltd
B1/I-1, Mohan Cooperative Industrial Area
Mathura Road, Post Bag 7
New Delhi 110044, India

E-mail us at **marketing@sagepub.in**

Subscribe to our mailing list
Write to **marketing@sagepub.in**

This book is also available as an e-book.

CONTENTS

LIST OF ILLUSTRATIONS

Figures

Tables

LIST OF ABBREVIATIONS

AAGSP	All Assam Gana Sangram Parishad
AAMSU	All Assam Minority Students' Union
AAMYP	All Assam Minority Yuva Parishad
AASU	All Assam Students' Union
ABMSU	All Bodoland Minority Students' Union
ABSU	All Bodo Students' Union
ABVP	Akhil Bharatiya Vidyarthi Parishad
ADCs	Autonomous District Councils
ADSF	Autonomy Demand Struggling Forum
AFSPA	Armed Forces (Special Powers) Act
AGP	Asom Gana Parishad
AGP(P)	Asom Gana Parishad (Progressive)
AGSP	Asom Gana Sangram Parishad
AICC	All India Congress Committee
AIUDF	All India United Democratic Front
AJS	Asom Jatiya Sanmilan
ALP	Asom Labour Party
APF	Assam People's Front
APHLC	All Party Hill Leaders Conference
ASDC	Autonomous State Demand Committee
ATTSA	All Assam Tea Tribes Students' Association
AUDF	Assam United Democratic Front
BJP	Bharatiya Janata Party
BJS	Bharatiya Jana Sangh
BPAC	Bodo People's Action Committee

BPF	Bodoland People's Front
BPPF	Bodoland People's Progressive Front
BPP(S)	Bodo People's Party (Sangsuma)
BTAD	Bodoland Territorial Autonomous District
BTC	Bodoland Territorial Council
CAB	Citizenship (Amendment) Bill
CPI	Communist Party of India
CPI(M)	Communist Party of India (Marxist)
CPI(ML)	Communist Party of India (Marxist–Leninist)
CRPC	Citizens' Right Preservation Committee
ESMA	Essential Services Maintenance Act
GoI	Government of India
IMDT Act	Illegal Migrants (Determination by Tribunal) Act
INC	Indian National Congress
INTUC	Indian National Trade Union Congress
JP	Janata Party
JS	Jana Sangh
LoC	Letter of credit
MoU	Memorandum of Understanding
NAGP	Natun Asom Gana Parishad
NDA	National Democratic Alliance
NEFA	North East Frontier Agency
NES	National Election Survey/Study
NRC	National Register of Citizens
NSCN	Nationalist Socialist Council of Nagaland
NSS	National Sample Survey
OBCs	Other Backward Castes/Classes
PDPA	People's Democratic Party of Assam
PLP	Purbanchaliya Lok Parishad
PTCA	Plain Tribes Council of Assam
RCPI	Revolutionary Communist Party of India
RSS	Rashtriya Swayam Sevak Sangh
SCs	Scheduled Castes
SLHEP	Subansiri Lower Hydroelectric Project
STs	Scheduled Tribes
SULFA	Surrendered United Liberation Front of Assam

ULFA	United Liberation Front of Assam
UMF	United Minority Front
UPP	United People's Party
UTNLF	United Tribal National Liberation Front
VHP	Vishwa Hindu Parishad
VKA	Vanavasi Kalyan Ashram

SERIES NOTE

The *SAGE Series on Politics in Indian States* aims at developing comprehensive, contemporary political histories of Indian states, looking
at the past two and a half decades. The series consists of volumes
covering important trends in the politics of major states of India.
Each volume, devoted to one particular state, situates the politics of
that state in the larger socio-historical context and presents a detailed
analysis of the significant patterns of competitive politics in the state
with a focus on framework of party competition, rise of new social
forces, role of leadership and the context of regional political economy.
Going beyond state-specificity, each volume also attempts to situate
the politics of the state in the larger all-India context.

Besides analysing the state-specific trends in party politics that
have led to the rise of many state parties, these volumes also care-
fully look at the social bases of parties and their electoral fortunes
in the backdrop of fluctuations in voter choices during elections of
the past quarter of a century, making use of the rich data archives
of Lokniti.

The unfolding dynamics of politics since the 1990s, which manifested at the state level at slightly different moments and sometimes
even preceded the 1990s, has forcefully brought back the states in
the consciousness of students of Indian politics. It has also led to
a renewed interest among sociologists and economists about the
political processes at state level and their interconnections with
socio-economic developments in India. At the same time, there is

a glaring absence of detailed documentations of the state-specific political processes during past two decades. The series addresses this gap in the literature on Indian politics. The series also propels more informed cross-state comparisons as a starting point to truly grasp 'all-India' politics.

ACKNOWLEDGEMENTS

We have incurred many debts to be recorded here while preparing this work. We would like to place on record our appreciation for the Lokniti programme of the Centre for the Study of Developing Societies (CSDS) Data Unit for generously allowing us to use their very rich pool of data. Professor Suhas Palshikar and Professor Rajeshwari Deshpande need a special mention for their continued support and help in editing the volume. This work would not have been possible but for the competent work of the team at SAGE Publications. We are extremely grateful to all of them.

INTRODUCTION

The map of Assam politics today appears to be strikingly different from what it was in the late 1980s. Politicization based on multiple social identities marks the politics of the state in this era. What catches the eye is the changing destiny of regional party, that is, Asom Gana Parishad (AGP), the revival and decline of the Congress party, and the Bharatiya Janata Party's (BJP) striking rise to power as an alternative to the Congress or regional party in the state. The notion that national parties have lost their relevance with the rise of the regional party in Assam seemed to have proved wrong in the state. Besides, what appears more startling is that issues that were central to the politics of the region during the pre-Partition days, such as land, immigration, language and identity continue to occupy major public space in the politics of the state, even after 70 years of Partition. Politics of the state primarily revolves around the issue of unchecked illegal migration from across the border since then. This book titled *Assam Politics in Post-Congress Era* is designed to unfold the nature of politics as it evolved in the post-1980s period.

The politics of Assam in the last decades serves as a textbook illustration of the complexities of the relationship between social cleavages and the competitive politics. Every professional or lay student of Assam politics would notice two fundamental changes: a 'fragmentation' of the party's political space and explosion of ethnicities in the arena of politics. The party system has changed from single-party dominance to a multiparty system that shows high degree of party fragmentation. The slow and somewhat dormant process of politicization has suddenly gathered momentum. It is hard to miss the link between these two processes: multiplication in the number of parties and politicization of multiple ethnicities. The state has moved from an era of catch-all formations to that of cleavage-based politics in extreme form and has witnessed multiplication in the number of political parties and politicization of multiple ethnicities. The multipolar nature of political competition has emerged with greater vehemence and clarity. Competitive politics undoubtedly creates and recreates imagined communities. The explosion of ethnicities in the arena of politics of the state illustrates this process. Realignment in the relationships among various kinds of pre-existing social cleavages has also emerged. The simultaneous operation of these alignments has made contemporary Assam a 'virtual laboratory of the politics of ethnicities'. The multipolar nature of political competition has emerged with greater vehemence and clarity now than ever before. However, the Politics of the state has taken an interesting turn at the end of the 20th century. What is unique about this state is that a number of ethnic groups has sought to create an exclusive politics of its own through the rise of many small, ethnicity-based political parties, unlike most other Indian states where regionalism is being articulated in terms of one dominant cultural community. Ironically, this has much to do with the success of the Assam Movement. However, the politics of Assamese nationalism accentuated the anxieties of not just the majority Assamese but also of all other ethnic groups. As a result, the major national parties have also defined their identity by appealing to specific social groups. The era of catch-all parties has given way to a political system based on social cleavages. The study covers the period from 1985 to 2019, which is marked by transition of power in the state (AGP to Congress and to BJP), leading to intense party competition and political mobilization based on ethnic and religious considerations.

The Assam Movement of 1979–1985 articulated the regional aspirations of the Assamese people, which energized the process of formation of a regional party, namely the AGP, as an alternative to the Congress party in the state in 1985. This was the first government by a regional party. The party held potent sway over the electorate for nearly two decades. However, the advantage secured by the AGP as a result of historical and political exigencies to unite the people of the state for forming a cohesive Assamese nationality could not be capitalized on by the party. It is now universally acknowledged that the party has failed to fulfil its historic role. Although, the AGP emerged as an alternative to the Congress and held its potent sway over the electorate for two decades, the political stagnation of the AGP marked the recovery of the Congress in the state in the late 1990s. The party managed to get majority in all the four Lok Sabha elections (1998–2009) and also in assembly elections for three consecutive terms. Yet the party has not been able to re-establish its dominance that it had in the pre-1985 era. The Congress party today is radically different from the Congress system. It is no longer the umbrella organization that covers all the various ethnicities and communities of the state. The result of the 2006 assembly elections for the first time compelled parties to form a coalition government in the state, which so far had always been ruled by a single party. The challenge put forward by the newly formed party—All India United Democratic Front (AIUDF)—to the monopoly of the Congress over the Muslim 'vote bank' is a new phenomenon in Assam politics since this election. Besides, the understanding between the AGP and the BJP has brought about a new equation in the electoral politics of the state. This shift in political preference has more to do with the fragmentation of political space and less with ideological concerns. Ideology and principle seem to have taken a back seat as political parties have opted for state-level alliances with the intent to bolster individual seat tallies. The 2014 Lok Sabha elections marked a withering of Congress dominance and the rise of the BJP in the state. In fact, Indian politics has entered a new era of Hindu nationalist hegemony fuelled by Modi's extraordinary popularity. As a result, a central gravitational force around which Indian politics revolves has become a reality. The BJP's electoral visibility in the state had been quite insignificant until the 2014 Lok Sabha elections. Since 1991 when it came to have a formal existence in the state, the maximum number of seats it could win in assembly or Lok Sabha elections was only five. Its influence did not extend beyond the urban areas of Assam. It was only in the wake of Assam Movement in 1978 that it started exerting its influence. Militant activities in the state also helped it to create a space for itself. The state has seen a remarkable paradigm shift in the trajectory of state politics with the landslide victory of the BJP in the assembly elections of 2016 and later in the 2019 Lok Sabha elections by ushering in a new phase of polarized politics in the state. The results amply reveal the changing nature of political dynamics in the state. Perhaps for the first time, the ethnic, regional and identity-based election issues have been sidelined, and those of governance and religion played a more important role in mobilizing voters. However, it is not easy to affirm that the troubled state is on the road to recovery. It depends on how well the party in power responds to and meets the dormant political desires of hitherto unrepresented social forces. True federalism with a commitment to constitutional processes can only recover the state from its present predicament. In the light of this perspective, the questions addressed in the book are: Why is politics in the state unique? Why could the Congress not sustain its dominance in the state? Has the AGP fulfilled the aspirations of the people of the state? Has the revival of the Congress in the late 1990s been earned by the party itself, or is it a by-product of the disarray within its opponents in the state? How have BJP's inroads into the state become possible?

Although there have been quite a few studies that deal with the situation as it evolved in the state during the later part of the 1980s with conceptual and theoretical interventions around the themes of identity, ethnicity and insurgency, no study has been conducted so far on the internal political processes of the state in the context of fundamental shifts that took place since the late 1980s onwards. This book is designed to address this existing gap in extant literature. Using the rich volume of data from the National Election Study/Survey (NES; CSDS), the study also attempts to answer many critical questions such as citizens' perception of state government, assessment of the government on major issues confronting the state, political preference among various communities and popularity level of political leadership.

THE DESIGN

This book contains seven chapters along with this introduction. Chapter 1, titled 'Politics of Assam: Background', introduces the state in terms of its location, geography, social plurality and economy. It also reflects on the development that took place in the colonial period, as these developments continue to have their effect on the politics of the state even today. Chapter 2, 'Congress Dominance and Decline', looks at the politics of the state since 1950 to the late 1970s. This was a period of Congress dominance in the state. Besides, it discusses how the politics of the state was shaped through the 1950s to the late 1970s is discussed. Immigration issue is one of the main props of the long Congress rule in the state. The electoral statistics clearly indicated the significant increase in the number of voters during this period mainly due to a large-scale influx of immigrant population. Besides, the illegal immigration of foreign nationals into Assam has serious political, cultural and economic implications. The 1977 'Janata Wave' had no impact on the electoral outcome of the state. When voters in most parts of India rejected the Congress party(I) of Indira Gandhi owing to the Emergency excesses, the electorate in the state gave the party 10 out of 14 seats in the Parliament with 50.6 per cent of total vote share. Congress's share of votes in the parliamentary elections, up to that period, remained above 45 per cent, and in the assembly elections, its lowest vote share during this period was 45.35 per cent. Some regional political groups and parties like All Party Hill Leaders Conference (APHLC) with non-Assamese-speaking ethnic support base began to do fairly well. But their influence was confined to select areas that were later carved out of Assam. Attempts to challenge the Congress by the People's Democratic Party and the Ujani Assam Rajya Parishad could not make any mark in the electoral politics of the state. The Congress had championed the cause of the Assamese national identity in terms of safeguarding Assamese language and culture during the pre-Independence period. This historical fact was in some way responsible for uninterrupted dominance of the Congress party in the political history of Assam from 1952 until 1978.

Chapter 3, 'Assam Movement and Its Fallout', reflects on the six-year-long Assam Movement and reveals how the movement was a political watershed for the Congress party.

Chapter 4, 'Asom Gana Parishad and Competitive Politics', high-lights how the politics of the state had taken an interesting turn since 1985, that significantly shaped the political history of the state. The 1985 election was a 'critical' election for Assam, for it led to a reconfiguration of the party system and a durable realignment of social groups with political parties. The regional aspirations of the Assamese people culminated in the formation of the regional party called the AGP in 1985. The AGP derived its strength from the perception of an imminent threat to the Assamese identity as a result of large-scale immigration. The anti-foreigner movement in Assam also led to the fragmentation of political space in the state. The movement gave expression to Assamese nationalism, and at the same time it spurred various subregional and ethnic aspira-tions which were given expression through the formation of several subregional parties. The AGP's inability to address the basic issues on which the party was formed, and its failure to adopt a clear-cut stand on the electoral alliance strategies since its emergence as a political force in the state, and more fundamentally its failure to fulfil its historic role of uniting all sections, including the unrep-resented social forces, to form a cohesive Assamese nationality are some of the factors that contributed to its downfall in the political arena.

The basic question raised in Chapter 5, 'Recovery of Congress', is whether the gains of the Congress party in the state were earned by the party itself or were the by-product of the disarray within its opponents. The Congress party's recovery in the state began in the late 1990s. The party consolidated its position significantly in both Lok Sabha and assembly elections. Although the party is back in power, it has been unable to re-establish the dominance that it lost in the pre-1985 era in terms of its vote share. The decline of Congress dominance in the state has been caused by the emergence of a multipolar party competition and the assertion and realignment of the ethnic identities. The entry of new social groups and parties has the potential of giving more meaning to competitive democracy in the state, yet this compe-tition has rarely led to better choices and new policies, programmes or institutional devices.

Chapter 6, 'Shift towards Bharatiya Janata Party', highlights on the causes through which BJP could make deep inroads into the state that had so far been seen as resistant to its charms, because the state had a strong regional party and also felt culturally distant from its emphasis on Hindutva. The BJP's rise to power in the 2016 assembly elections has made political history with the changing nature of political dynamics in the state. The mandate is seen as the voters seeking a change to end troubles towards good governance and the development of the state. The promise will have to be fulfilled in the time to come for the troubles of the state to recede. The Congress's three consecutive terms have failed to show evidence of fulfilling the above expectations. What is more significant is that the voters in 2016 assembly elections have delivered a clear mandate. The election result in the state reminds one of a similar poll upheaval in 1985 when the regional party AGP made history, all by itself, by overthrowing the Congress. Interestingly, some of the stalwarts of the then AGP, including its president Prafulla Mahanta, who subsequently became the chief minister for two terms, are at present in alliance with the BJP. The common chord that seems to bind the two parties, including other ethnic partners, is the guarantee of security to the indigenous people, settling the foreigners' issue and sealing the Indo-Bangla border. With the BJP being in power at the Centre and the above issues remaining almost unaddressed in the state, the voters may have considered the present chemistry between the regional and national party as a potential way to resolve the lingering tangle. This inner logic may have prompted them to remain in proximity with the central government. In spite of this massive victory, it is too early to affirm that the troubled state would be on the road to recovery. The future of the BJP will depend less on short-term political exigencies and more on how well they respond to and meet the dormant political desires of hitherto unrepresented social forces under the larger federal political umbrella that can effectively strike a balance between the ruling segments and the minorities.

Chapter 7, 'Challenges Ahead', gives an overview of the work, highlighting the pattern of changes in the political dynamics of the state.

The present book is the product of many years of work of the author. The field research to the same dates back to late 1996, when the author was associated with NES. At the initiative of the Lokniti programme at CSDS, a series of election surveys for both assembly and Lok Sabha, in the form of pre-poll, mid-poll and post-poll surveys, are being carried out at regular intervals in Assam. The large volume of empirical data generated through these surveys have been used for the study.

Politics of Assam

Background

The specificities of political dynamics in Assam varies compared to other states in India. Assam presents a unique fusion of different racial and linguistic elements. It is a classic case of composite culture emerging out of migration over the centuries. The long-term migratory flow into the state makes it linguistically and ethnically the most diversified state in India. In fact, diverse communities in the state, with striking differences in their origin, language and religion lead to the rise of conflicts and contestation of power, with each group perceiving the 'other' as a threat to its existence. For creating and consolidating their respective identities, every ethnic group makes effort to construct its 'other'. The ideology of 'the other' actually motivates and guides identity politics in the state. Although patterns of ethnicity worldwide present striking similarities, every situation of ethnicity has historical and contextual specificities. In particular, every situation of ethnic nationalism has a threshold that enables a before-and-after type analysis. Assam is a classic case of a composite culture that has emerged out of migration over the centuries. Successive governments at the centre, while fully aware of the consequences faced by the state, because of illegal immigration, failed in their obligation to protect the border as well as the rights of the genuine citizens. As a consequence, the cultural processes, values and practices of ethnic groups have increasingly become political resources for various parties in their competition for political power or economic advantage. Politics over citizenship issue as a result of migration and identity question makes the state quite distinct from other states in India. The persistence of insurgency in the state, as well as the proliferation of the militant outfits, is a phenomenon, although in a low intensity in recent times, that has no parallel elsewhere in India.

GEOGRAPHICAL LOCATION

Assam occupies a strategic position in the political map of India by virtue of its geographical location. The state shares its borders in the north with five states, namely Arunachal Pradesh, Nagaland, Manipur, Mizoram and Meghalaya and one country, namely Bhutan. On its western boundary lies West Bengal, Tripura and Bangladesh, with 2,276.3 km interstate and 529 km of international borders. With an area of 78.438 sq. km, Assam represents 2.4 per cent of the total geographical area of India. The geographical terrain of the state has a mix of hill and plain districts. Out of total 27 districts, two, namely Karbi Anglong and Dima Hasao, are hill districts. The plains are divided into two valleys—the Brahmaputra and the Barak valleys—each having unique historical legacies. The Brahmaputra Valley is further divided into two banks—southern and northern. Also, the valley is divided as 'upper' and 'lower' with respect to the course of the river Brahmaputra. The history of the divisions is distinct in terms of population settlement and agricultural practices, giving rise to unique social and economic formations in the districts (Assam Human Development Report; Government of Assam 2014).

NATURE OF DIVERSITY

Assam is known as the melting pot of diverse cultural streams, namely the Indo-Aryan, the Austro-Mongoloid and the Indo-Iranian. Diversities in terms of ethnic origins, linguistic variation and religious pluralism characterize this region. The complex and overlapping nature of diversity determines the nature of politics in the state. Just as there is 'religious' diversity between Hindus and Muslims, there are also linguistic diversities among the subgroups of both these communities. Therefore, it is not easy to privilege any one on the basis of diversity over all others. Major components of the state's social mosaic are Hindus (61.5%) and Muslims (34.2%) of the total population of the state (Table 1.1). Muslims are in majority in 9 out of 27 districts of the state (Table 1.2). The state has three major groups of Muslims: Assamese-speaking Muslims, whose ancestors date back to the 13th century, then Muslims of Bangla origin, and the post-1971 Bangladeshi

Table 1.1 Demography of Assam (in Percentage)

Hindu	Muslim	Christian	Sikh	Buddhist	Jain	Other Religions
61.47	34.22	3.74	0.07	0.18	0.08	0.09

Source: Census 2011, Assam.

Table 1.2 Religious Demography in Assam (District-wise)

District	Hindu (%)	Muslim (%)	Others (%)
Baksa	82.40	14.29	3.31
Barpeta	29.11	70.74	0.15
Bongaigaon	48.61	50.22	1.17
Cachar	59.83	37.71	2.46
Chirang	66.50	22.66	10.84
Darang	35.25	64.34	0.41
Dhemaji	95.47	1.96	2.57
Dhubri	19.92	79.67	0.41
Dibrugarh	90.35	4.86	4.79
Dima Hasao	67.07	2.04	30.89
Goalpara	34.51	57.52	7.97
Golaghat	85.99	8.46	5.55
Hailakandi	38.10	60.31	1.59
Jorhat	92.31	5.01	2.89
Kamrup	57.82	39.66	2.52
Kamrup (M)	84.89	12.05	3.06
Karbi Anglong	80.10	2.12	17.78
Karimganj	42.48	56.36	1.16
Kokrajhar	59.64	28.44	11.92
Lakhimpur	76.49	18.57	4.94
Morigaon	47.20	52.56	0.24
Nagaon	43.39	55.36	1.25
Nalbari	63.71	35.96	0.33
Sivasagar	87.51	8.30	4.19
Sonitpur	73.95	18.22	7.83
Tinsukia	88.96	3.64	7.4
Udalguri	73.64	12.66	13.7

Source: Census 2011, Assam.

Muslims. The Muslims are the largest minority community and by and large play a decisive role in the politics in Assam.

In terms of language, the major linguistic groups are Assamese (48.3%) and Bengali (29%; Census 2011). The Bengalis form a majority in the Barak Valley districts, namely Cachar, Karimganj and Hailakandi. The Scheduled Castes (SCs) and Scheduled Tribes (STs) form an important component of Assam's demography, society and polity. The SC and ST populations are 7.15 per cent and 12.44 per cent, respectively (Census 2011). The STs mostly belong to the Tibeto-Burman ethnolinguistic group. Besides this major group, another group called Austro-Asiatic (Mon-Khmer-speaking Khasis and Mundari-speaking Munda, Santhal, Ho Aron, etc.) forms a small segment of the state's tribal population. Among the various tribal communities of Assam, Bodo (belonging to the Bodo-Kachari ethnolinguistic group), Mishing, Kachari including Sonowal, Karbi, Dimasa, Rabha, Deoris and Tiwa are the major tribes in terms of numerical strength. With regard to the distribution pattern of tribal people, except for Karbi and Dimasa (hill tribes) living mostly in the Karbi Anglong district, the rest live in the plains and are concentrated in distinct areas of the state. The Karbis and Dimasa Kacharis live in the two hill districts, namely Karbi Anglong and North Cachar. The population in Assam is also further divided in terms of multiple communities or subnationalities, such as immigrant Muslims, Hindus, Nepalese and tea-tribe communities. The linguistic, religious and ethnic diversity not only creates a tremendous scope for sociocultural overlap but also political polarization on ethnic lines. The trends of politics and the nature of political competition in the state reflect the political significance of its multi-ethnic reality (Figure 1.1).

Apart from strategic location and unique diversities, the state is also characterized by varied institutional arrangements of governance. The two hill districts of the state have Autonomous District Councils (ADCs) formed under the provisions of the Sixth Schedule of the Constitution. Further, through an amendment to the Sixth Schedule in 2003, four districts, namely Kokrajhar, Baksa, Chirang and Udalguri, have been incorporated as the Bodoland Territorial Autonomous District (BTAD) and brought under the Bodoland Territorial Council (BTC).

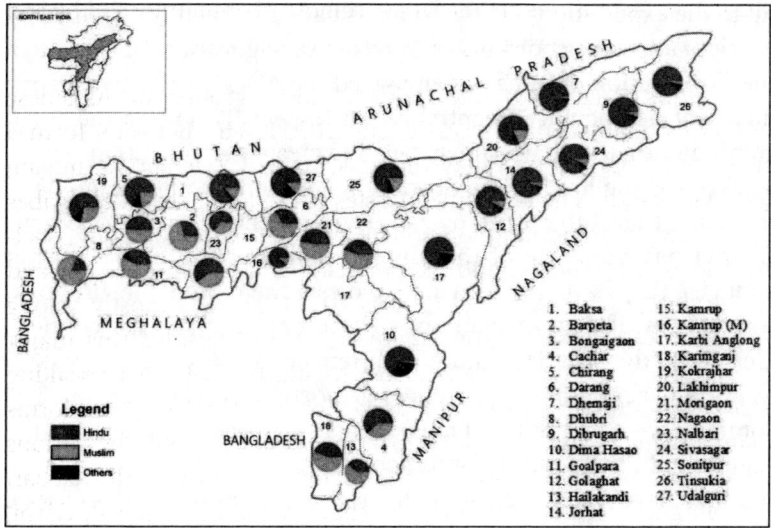

Figure 1.1 *Ethnic Composition of Assam, 2011*

Source: Census data 2011, Assam.

Disclaimer: This figure has been redrawn and is not to scale. It does not represent any authentic national or international boundaries and is used for illustrative purposes only.

The rest of the districts in the state are under Part IX of the Constitution, where panchayats and urban local bodies are functional. Besides, six autonomous councils were formed through state legislations for six communities, namely Rabha-Hasong, Mishing, Tiwa, Deori, Thengal Kachari and Sonowal Kachari. Moreover, 18 community-specific development councils were created by the state government, which are primarily mandated to focus on development of specific communities. ADCs, including the BTC, created under the Sixth Schedule of the Constitution have detailed functions and powers in the legislature, executive, judicial and financial domains. These powers are expected to uplift the tribal communities, especially in the domains of primary education, health, culture, social customs, social welfare, forest, land, agriculture, water management, village administration and economic and rural development. However, in practice, the performance of the autonomous councils has not been up to the expectations. These councils have also been constrained by a lack of adequate coordination with the state government. Although the Constitution of India has envisaged the ADCs as effective instruments of democratic decentralization, especially among the tribal communities, they have largely failed to create the institutions envisaged below the level of the district. In addition, though planning at the district level to ensure overall development of the Autonomous District has been one of the fundamental concerns of the district councils, they have not been able to create the required institutional mechanism of district planning. The other autonomous councils created by the state legislature have remained substantially weak in terms of ushering in the process of democratic decentralization. The community-centric autonomous councils witness a tendency of the state to fulfil the political aspirations of the respective communities, but they have never been strengthened as institutions of democratic decentralization ensuring people's participation at the grassroots. The other development councils which are again community-centric have also never been operationalized with the ethos of democratic decentralization and remain dependent on the mercy of the state government. These institutions have also not been able to involve the community at large. Similar failure is also eminent in the panchayats. The actual devolution of funds, functionaries and functions is still inadequate in the panchayats. The District Planning Committees lack effectiveness in district planning exercises. These shortcomings have clear implications for the overall governance structure and outcome in the state (Assam Human Development Report; Government of Assam 2014).

HISTORICAL BACKGROUND

Assam was originally ruled by Ahoms, an offshoot of the Tai or the great Shan stock of Southeast Asia, prior to the advent of British rule. The Ahoms ruled Assam for a little less than 600 years. The society in Assam, prior to the coming of the British, was semi-tribal–feudal in structure. The India system of feudalism could never infiltrate deeply into the major parts of Assam and hence never posed a challenge to the Ahom system of government. Hinduism being the dominant religion, the traditional division of the society into different categories of caste existed (Deka 1973). The political scenario of Assam underwent change during the Ahom rule, and their influence on the social practices was much pronounced. At that time, Tantric cult or Saktism prevailed and had long-lasting influence on the people of Assam. Worshiping many gods and goddesses, practice of animal sacrifice (even human sacrifice in certain places) and maintenance of caste hierarchy prevailed throughout Assam. Sankaradeva propagated neo-Vaishnavism at a time when ritualism was gaining firm impact, with occasional intrusion of ultrareligious animism and occultism. However, as Sankaradeva started propagating his philosophy of *ek-sarana-naam-dharma*, the dogma of polytheism started moving to a belief system of one God and his avatars, especially Krishna and Rama. This belief system replaced sacrificial rites, and prayer, devotion and meditation were followed and persuaded in its doctrines. Internal dissension in the later period of Ahom rule instigated Burmese conquest in 1819, and finally in 1826 it was put to rout by the British.

The period since 1826 up until the British rulers left India in 1947 was a formative epoch in the political history of Assam. It marked not only the end of the independent and powerful Ahom monarchy but paved the way for a new regime of foreign domination, the effects of which can be felt even today. In this process, the land of different tribal people, who inhabited the hilly and forest-infested tracts of the northeast region, was annexed by the British rulers and added on to the already extensive area of Assam proper. This led to further diversifying the sociocultural situation in Assam. The other element that added to the diversification of the Assamese social contour was the influx of immigrants from outside the borders of Assam province. The process of colonization in Assam aimed at restructuring the society and monetizing its economy to serve the imperial interests (Goswami 1997, 13). The process of territorial adjustments and readjustments also had its impact on the economic, political, sociocultural and demographic aspects of Assam.

WAVES OF MIGRATION IN THE COLONIAL PERIOD

The colonial rulers had opened the doors of Assam to immigration to suit their own commercial interests. The closed society was exposed to immigration labour, new skills and new ideas. The immigration has done much towards opening out and closing the fertile and sparsely peopled districts of Assam while relieving other provinces of substantial portion of their surplus population. The establishment of the Assam Tea Company was part of the scheme of colonizing wasteland in Assam to provide new avenues of investment for foreign capital (Guha 1968). The tea industry required a regular supply of labour. With minimal capital investment, the British entrepreneurs reaped large benefits by paying abnormally low wages to the labourers brought almost as slaves from the poverty-stricken areas of Bihar, Orissa and the Madras Presidency. Although initially the local Assamese people were employed as labourers, the practice was later discontinued due to signs of rebellion and discontentment among the Assamese labourers in the early years of the plantation days. Immigrant labourers could be exploited and ill-treated without much impact on the surrounding villages. The British rulers, therefore, encouraged large-scale immigration into Assam tea gardens. Thousands of labourers were annually recruited for the plantations from other provinces. Most of whom did not return home and formed the biggest migrant group in Assam's population.

The other strand of imperialist policy in Assam was to suppress local languages and set up artificial boundaries for the sake of a cheap and simplified administration. This policy affected the local middle class and by promoting differences between them and the immigrants, it served as an instrument of 'divide and rule'. Assamese language remained suppressed in Assam during the whole period from 1836 to 1871, and this decision on the language question struck a severe blow to the nascent Assamese nationalism and even endangered the survival of Assamese nationality. The initial monopoly of office in almost all the departments by the newcomers from Bengal naturally generated ill-feeling and deep resentment among those for whom hitherto there was no means of livelihood other than government service. The polemic between the Bengali and Assamese languages since then has been fairly continuous and symbolizes in many ways the fight between the interests of an immigrant and comparatively advanced middle class on the one hand, and an indigenous less advanced and suppressed middle class on the other hand. In the first decade of this century, the Bengali middle class had already produced a big surplus of educated youth who could not hope to be employed in their narrow provincial set-up. They sought their fortunes in the neighbouring states of Orissa, Bihar and Assam where their assertion of cultural superiority exacerbated resentment at their success in finding jobs (Broomfield 1968).

The immigration of the Muslim peasants into Assam in the first decade of this century was clearly linked with the growth of the jute industry in and around Calcutta run by British finance capital. With the expansion of the jute trade, the stepping up of jute cultivation also became an immediate necessary. As the area of jute cultivation in Bengal could no longer be extended, it was thought suitable to grow jute in Assam. As a result, the immigration of expert jute cultivators into Assam started. Besides, Bengal had been the scene of mounting peasant mobilization against the zamindari oppression and exploitation (Guha 1968). Therefore, immigration into Assam from East Bengal was encouraged under landlord–imperialist machination. This process had two immediate effects. First, it resulted in the ebb, though temporary, of peasant upsurge in Bengal and, second, it created a situation of conflict between the Assamese and Bengali peasants. The exploiting landlords and their overloads realized that their interests would be served as long as there was disunity among the toiling masses in the name of language, religion and nationality (Guha 1965).

The increase in the migration of Muslim peasants from East Bengal between 1911 and 1921 was characterized by a gradual spread of Muslim immigrants up the Brahmaputra Valley. But during the decade of 1911–1921 the agricultural expansion was extended far up the valley and the Muslim immigrants came to form an appreciable part of the population in all the four lower and central districts. Only the two Upper Assam districts, Sivasagar and Lakhimpur, remained practically untouched. One added attraction for these immigrants from East Bengal to come to Assam was the Ryotwari land tenure system in Assam, which offered them the taste of a refreshing life of peasant proprietorship in sharp contrast to the Permanent Settlement system of East Bengal. An open-door policy followed by the British in a linguistic subregion apparently led to a dangerous situation for the local community (Guha 1968) of being culturally swamped or demographically outnumbered by a dominant and numerous community.

The constant public pressure against the migration, the officials of Nowgong district finally devised an administrative measure known as the Line System to restrict the indiscriminate settlement by immigrants in the Assamese-inhabited areas in 1916. However, the authorities did not maintain the authenticity of the Line System, and the government's scheme and methods regarding the legitimate settlement of the immigrants appeared important as strict observance was not maintained by the authorities. The government's intention was not to stop the inflow of immigrants but to put effective administrative control on the settlement areas to derive more revenue benefits. Added to these considerations, several political factors were responsible. The Muslim League government (1939–1946 with interruption), which controlled the state before and during the Second World War, allowed and even encouraged Muslim immigrants which later on matured into a demand for the inclusion of the entire province of Assam into Pakistan (Bhuyan and De 1978, 64–65). This large-scale immigration led to a shift in the demographic balance in favour of the Muslims with abnormal rise in their proportion and soon it became a serious concern for the Assamese intelligentsia that if immigration continued at the same pace, the Assamese-speaking people would ultimately turn into a linguistic minority in their own land. Realizing the seriousness of the problem, Jawaharlal Nehru during his visit to Assam in 1937 as the Congress President commented, 'The immigration question is a complicated one. Essentially it is an economic question and it would be tackled in an economic way. The desire of the Assamese people to preserve their language is perfectly legitimate'. Emphasizing on the process of assimilation of these immigrants, he observed that the immigrants should always be assimilated; otherwise they become foreign bodies always giving trouble. The noted historian Amalendu Guha noted:

> If the immigration continued unrestrained, would not the Assamese be turned into a linguistic minority in their own home? He further added that an open door policy towards migrants, therefore, might be unwise from another point of view, particularly so, when in a small linguistic subregion such immigration leads to the danger of the local community being culturally swamped or outnumbered by another dominant or numerous community. (Guha 1977)

On the whole, British rule ingeniously created animosity among people of different nationalities and religious beliefs and governed them through a 'divide and rule' policy. The economic changes that were introduced in the united Assam–Bengal province under colonization had a disintegration effect on the relations between the Assamese and the Bengali communities. This provided, as it historically did in most parts in India, a specific arc where politics could be manipulated.

Assam lagged behind the more advanced parts of India during the medieval times due to a low level of economic development, its geographical considerations and the isolationist policy of the Ahom monarchy. The downfall of the feudal order did not bring the pace of development in Assam in line with that of the rest of British India. There was no native capitalist in Assam. This explains the commercial monopoly of Marwari merchants who followed the British into Assam and diligently tapped the available few opportunities for money making, opened by the British, like money lending, supplying provisions to the tea gardens, procuring mustard and later jute for the market outside Assam, and meeting the demand for new household implements and articles—cheap and mass produced—that the Assamese soon came to adopt. On the whole, imperialism acted as a further brake on the development forces of production, communication, and education and political consciousness also suffered from a corresponding stagnation. The economic weakness and political immaturity of the middle class continued to prevent it from having a decisive confrontation with big capital which succeeded imperialism as the main exploiter, though the middle class had some gains since Independence (Barua 1974).

DEMOGRAPHIC CHANGE AFTER INDEPENDENCE

The decades after Independence marked a new phase of demographic development in the state. The size and rate of increase of population is an important factor in the ethnic conflicts in Assam. Actually, there were two sides to the migration issue. One was Bengali Hindu refugees who were taking shelter in Assam following partition and became an important factor in the politics of the state. The other was illegal

Muslim immigration from East Pakistan. The post-1947 immigration has brought about major demographic changes in several districts of the state and this has naturally altered the political equations of the state and has added a new dimension to Assam's demographic balance. But the most important question is the pressure on land, which is at the core of indigenous identity and which one feels to be the marked feature of such immigration. This is a much more basic issue, calling into question one of the defining characteristics of a nationality: territory and loss of territory to people who settle on it, which tends to be permanent. This is a problem that distinguishes the Assam situation from any other part of India (Omvedt 1980). Yet, the land factor has not received the due attention that it deserves from successive governments in the state. The high rate of population growth in Assam is not due to high birth rate or low death rate. Rather it is due to a large-scale immigration since the beginning of the British rule from outside the country, and later mainly from the then East Pakistan and from other states of India. P. C. Goswami traces the origin of these human waves to three main centres, namely (a) from Bihar, Uttar Pradesh (UP), Orissa and Madras as labourers who came to Assam for working in tea gardens; (b) from East Pakistan as settlers on agricultural land and (c) from Nepal as livestock farmers. Added to this, there has been a steady inflow of East Bengal Hindu refugees since Independence. Apart from these, a large number of people from other states also came to Assam to earn their livelihood as traders, labourers and salary earners. In a society, where there is private ownership over land and other means of production is very limited, such a massive influx of homeless people inevitably creates pressure on the economic system and drives the local people to enter into stiff competition for living. As a result, discontent against the people seeking shelter in Assam is generated among local people. If the then state government was sincere enough to exercise even a part of the power granted to it by the Immigrants (Expulsion from Assam) Act, 1950, Assam could have been saved from the present predicament. In this connection Myron Wiener's comment is worth quoting:

> In neighbouring Tripura, a state dominated both politically and demographically by Bengali Hindus, the immigration act was enforced, resulting

in a substantial return of immigrated Bengali Muslim to East Pakistan between 1961 and 1971, as reflected in an absolute decline in the Muslim population from 230,000 in 1961 to 103,000 in 1971. (Weiner and Katzestein 1981)

In the absence of any such positive step, Assam continued to be a coveted Lebensraum for the illegal immigrants. Analysing the demographic changes in Assam during the period of 1901–1971, the Census of India 1971 made the observation that, 'taking the whole population of 3.29 million of Assam in 1901 as indigenous and applying the all India rate of increase of 129.67 per cent from 1901 to 1971, her population in 1971 could be 7.56 million instead of 34.63 million. Although the 1981 census could not be held in Assam, her population in 1981, at the rate of growth of 34.95 per cent recorded in 1971, can be estimated at 19.7 million. The discrepancy between the above two estimates may be attributed mainly to the presence of an excess population of illegal immigrants from Bangladesh' (Census 1971). Although, under the law of the land, alliance cannot be allowed to decide the political destiny of any state or the country, this is precisely what has happened in the case of Assam. This fact was indeed realized by the central government as early as 1963 when in a document released by it, the observation about the influx infiltration from East Pakistan was made that the enlistment of foreigners has at times taken place at the instance of politically interested persons or parties.[1] Political parties have been known to take dubious steps to inflate the number of their supporters at election times and some undoubtedly used the illegal settlers from Bangladesh towards this end. The mere fact that a person's name is rightly or wrongly inscribed on the voters' list does not prove or confer Indian nationality and citizenship. This legal position has been confirmed by decisions of the Supreme Court of India. In 1971, the Chief Election Commissioner of India, referring to the alarming situation in Assam especially among the states of Northeast India, does expressed[2]:

[1] Ministry of Information and Broadcasting, Government of India, August 1963.

[2] Conference of Election Officers, Ootacamund, 24–26 September 1978.

In one case, that is (Assam), the population in 1971 census recorded an increase as high as 34.98 per cent over the 1961 Census figures and this increase was attributed to the influx of a very large number of persons from the neighbouring countries. The influx has become a regular feature. I think that it may not be a wrong assessment to make that on the basis of increase of 34.98 per cent between the two censuses, the increase that is likely to be recorded in 1991 Census would be more over that of the 1961 Census. In other words, a stage would be reached when that state might have to reckon with the foreign nationals who may, in all probability, constitute a sizeable percentage if not the majority of the population of the state.

Further, he was also very critical about the role of political parties vis-à-vis the foreigner issue. Another disturbing factor in this regard is the demand made by the political parties for the inclusion in the electoral roles of the names of such migrants who are not Indian citizens without even questioning and properly determining their citizenship status. This is a serious affair. The gravity of the situation, therefore, calls for drastic and effective measures; however, in reality no such measures were taken and it was precisely because of the government's failure to deal with the silent invasion by the foreign nationals that a massive popular movement started in Assam from 1979 onwards demanding revision of the voters' list, followed by detection and deportation of the foreign nationals. The growth rate of population in the state was higher than the all-India average till 1991; however, since 1991–2001 it has reduced than all India average (Table 1.3).

ECONOMY

Assam is predominantly an agricultural state. Agriculture is the mainstay of a majority of the population. Wet rice is mostly practised in the valley region. The Census 2011 data reveal that about 50 per cent of the total workforce (main and marginal put together) are still engaged in agriculture. Development of agriculture is, therefore, vital to strengthen the economy of Assam. If all potentialities of agricultural development in the state can be explored, Assam can in fact be made the food grain basket for the whole of northeast region of India while

Table 1.3 *Population Growth Rate in Assam and India*

States	1941–1951	1951–1961	1961–1971	1981–1991	1991–2001	2001–2011
Assam	19.93	34.98	34.95[a]	24.24	18.92	16.90
Andhra Pradesh	14.02	15.65	20.90	24.20	14.59	11.10
Bihar	10.27	19.78	21.31	23.54	28.62	25.07
Orissa	6.38	19.82	25.05	20.06	16.25	14.00
West Bengal	13.22	21.79	26.89	24.75	17.77	13.93
Kerala	22.62	24.76	26.79	26.39	9.43	4.90
Tamil Nadu	14.66	11.85	22.39	15.39	11.72	15.60
All India	13.03	21.60	24.80	23.87	21.54	17.64

Source: Census of India, Series 1 (Assam) India.

Notes: [a]Including Meghalaya; 1981 Census could not be held in Assam.

developing a regional food security grid.[3] However, the state has remained bogged down with enormous problems that have slowed down its march towards higher level of agricultural production and productivity. Although modern technological innovation in agriculture has been ushered in most of the states in India to accelerate the growth rate, Assam seems to have lagged far behind even in this respect. The infrastructural facilities for agricultural development in Assam are poor and the age-old methods of cultivation are still in operation. One of the major problems of agricultural development, in particular, and economic backwardness, in general, for Assam is the occurrence of recurrent floods every year. Floods in Assam cause serious soil erosion, loss of life and livestock and heavy damage to infrastructure and property, thereby retarding agricultural productivity. The recurrence of flood and erosion continue to be the burning problems of the state. The greatest single casualty of the recurrent floods is the agricultural sector—the mainstay of the state economy.

An important feature revealed by the Agricultural Census is that the average size of operational holdings in the state recorded a declining

[3] Shukla Committee report.

trend over the successive censuses. For example, the average size of operational holdings, which was 1.47 hectares in 1970–1971, recorded decline to 1.10 hectares in 2010–2011 (Table 1.4). The proportion of land under cultivation is quite small and the area which can be brought under cultivation is also limited. With gradual shrinking of agricultural land due to growth of population, flood, erosion and conversion for non-agricultural purposes, it is all the more imperative for the state to go for multiple cropping pattern and technological innovations for sustaining high agricultural growth like some states in India.

The state government has made some interventions recently through chief minister's 'Samagra Gramya Yojana' which aims at doubling the farmer's income within 2022 in consonance with nation-wide programme for the same purpose. Besides, some interventions are reported to have been made in terms of technological assistance, market linkage, institutional finance, etc. However, results so far have not been found encouraging. The farmer community's well-being is intrinsically related to having proper village infrastructure in addition

Table 1.4 Agricultural Holdings and Operated Area in Assam (as per Agricultural Censuses)

Agricultural Census Year	Number of Holdings (in '000)	Total Operated Area (in Thousand Hectare)	Average Size of Holdings (in Hectare)
1970–1971	1964.38	2,882	1.47
1976–1977	2254.65	3,079	1.37
1980–1981	2298.59	3,121	1.36
1985–1986	2419.16	3,161	1.31
1990–1991	2523.38	3,205	1.27
1995–1996	2683.00	3,138	1.17
2000–2001	2712.14	3,114	1.15
2005–2006	2750.11	3,049	1.11
2010–2011	2720.22	2,999	1.10

Source: Directorate of Economics and Statistics, Assam.

Note: Total may not be equal due to rounding off to nearest zero.

to agro-related amenities. An all-encompassing holistic approach, therefore, can take care of the varied aspects that are linked to an inclusive agricultural growth [*The Assam Tribune* (Editorial) 2019]. A holistic analysis could proceed from the study of society, rather than individuals, and assume that individual behaviour is determined by the social whole, rather than the converse. Agricultural risks affect production and farmers' livelihoods at a broader level. Besides, risks faced by agricultural stakeholders are numerous and are often context-specific. Risk is composed of three elements: threat, uncertainty and loss. In this sense, risk is the threat of loss or damage caused by an unfavourable event which is uncertain. The uncertain event can be the result of either natural hazards or human activities or both. A holistic approach to agricultural risks means to consider a broad range of risks and hence a broad range of solutions, and that no risk is considered in isolation. For risks that cannot be mitigated or transferred, coping strategies come into play. Particularly important is the role of government in formulating appropriate coping mechanisms to deal with such matters at catastrophic levels as a key component in the resilience of vulnerable stakeholders.

The state has a predominant place in cultivation and production of tea in India. Assam has been well known internationally in this sector since long. The total number of large tea gardens is 765 with 233 lakh hectares of area under their possession. The tea gardens represent a typical diversity with distinct population streams that migrated into the state during the colonial period. Life and livelihood at the tea garden are characterized by the typical features of plantation economy (Assam Human Development Report 2014). The tea-tribe communities are an important section of Assamese society and they constitute almost 20 per cent of the state's population. They belong to a cluster of about 114 tribal groups. The tea-tribe communities continue to experience social exclusion in social, political and economic walks even today. Wage is one important issue of contention between the worker and the management. Although a memorandum of settlement has been signed between five management groups on 26 June 2012, yet the tea plantation workers are still being paid wages below the minimum wages of agricultural workers. There has not been much improvement in their education, health, economic and political status. Though they are politically integrated and they actively participate in the electoral politics, they lack effective leadership to represent their grievances to the state. Assam is also widely known for its abundant mineral resources, mainly petroleum (crude), natural gas (utilized), coal and limestone. However, due to non-utilization of natural gas and the by-products of the crude refined oil in Assam, no ancillary industries worth the name have been set up in Assam. Despite possessing such a valuable resource, Assam's economy, unlike the oil-rich countries, continues to remain underdeveloped and Assam continues to lag behind in respect of per capita income at the national level every year. For example, the per capita income of the state even during the period of 2016–2017 remained below the national average (Table 1.5).

Table 1.5 *Per Capita Income (in ₹) of the State and India*

	At Current Price		At Constant Price	
Year	Assam	India	Assam	India
1980–1981[a]	1,673	1,852	9,334	10,712
1990–1991[a]	5,315	5,621	10,915	14,330
2000–2001[a]	12,803	17,295	12,447	20,362
2004–2005[b]	16,782	24,143	16,782	24,143
2008–2009[b]	24,099	40,775	18,922	31,754
2009–2010[b]	28,383	46,249	20,406	33,901
2010–2011[b]	33,087	54,021	21,146	36,342
2011–2012[c]	41,142	63,460	41,142	63,460
2012–2013[c]	44,599	71,050	41,609	65,664
2013–2014[c]	49,734	79,412	43,002	68,867
2014–2015[c]	52,895	86,879	44,809	72,889
2015–2016[c]	60,526(PE)	93,293	48,725(PE)	77,435
2016–2017[c]	65,698(QE)	103,219(PE)	51,040(QE)	82,269(PE)

Source: Directorate of Economics and Statistics, Assam and Central Statistics Office (MOSPI), Government of India.

Notes: [a] From 1980–1981 to 2000–2001, the base year is 1999–2000; [b] from 2004–2005 to 2010–2011, the base year is 2004–2005; [c] from 2011–2012 to 2016–2017, the base year is 2011–2012.

This chapter presents a broad overview of the socio-economic situation of Assam and also throws light on how the politics in the state has its root in its historical past. In the next chapter, we explore the major issues around which the state politics had been entangled during the period of Congress dominance.

REFERENCES

Assam Human Development Report. 2014. 'Managing Diversities, Achieving Human Development'.

Bhuyan, A. C., and Shibapada De. 1978. *Guwahati. Political History of Assam*. Vol. 2. Guwahati: Government of Assam.

Broomfield, J. H. 1968. *Elite Conflict in a Plural Society*. Berkeley, CA: University of California.

Census 2011. 2011 Census Data. Available at: http://censusindia.gov.in/2011-Common/CensusData2011.html

Deka, K. 1973. 'Structural Changes during the British Regime'. *North Eastern Research Bulletin* IV.

Dutta, Nandana. 2012. *Questions of Identity in Assam: Location, Migration, Hybridity*. New Delhi: SAGE Publications.

Goswami, Sandhya. 1997. *Language Politics in Assam*. New Delhi: Ajanta Publications.

Government of Assam. 2014. *Assam Human Development Report 2014: Managing Diversities, Achieving Human Development*. Guwahati: Government of Assam.

Guha, Amalendu. 1965. 'Socio-economic Changes in Agrarian Assam'. In *Trends in Socio-economic Change in India: 1871–1961*, edited by M. K. Chowdhary. Simla: Indian Institute of Advanced Study.

———. 1968. 'Impact of Bengal Renaissance on Assam: 1826–1876'. *Indian Social and Economic History Review* 5 (2, June): 125–148.

———. 1977. *Planter Raj to Swaraj: Freedom Struggle & Electoral Politics in Assam 1826–1947*. New Delhi: People's Publishing House.

Omvedt, Gail. 1980. 'Aspects of the Assamese Problem'. *Frontier*, 7 June.

Roy, Ramashray, Sujata Miri, and Sandhya Goswami. 2007. *Northeast India: Development, Communalism and Insurgency*. New Delhi: Anshah.

Swaminathan, M. S. 2001. 'Livelihood Security Must Be Bottomline'. *Frontline*, 3–16 February.

The Assam Tribune (Editorial), 'A Holistic Approach', October 2019.

Congress Dominance and Decline

The Congress party is historically known for its hegemonic role in the political history of Assam. The party had significantly built itself on a solid foundation during the nationalist movement. The Congress party's role as the ruling party in the state of Assam for a very long time makes it distinct from most other states in India. The dominance of Congress in the politics of Assam continued uninterrupted for three decades, beginning with the first election in 1952 after Independence. The late 1980s was a critical period for the Congress party in the state though it came back to power in 2001 with a majority and then remained in power for three consecutive terms. In the initial phase from 1952 to 1977, Congress never faced any electoral upset in the state. No political party or formation came close to challenging the dominance of Congress party in the state. The Congress party was able to manage their mutual differences very skilfully in spite of having various factions within the party.

While discussing the politics of the state of Assam, it is important to refer to the major issues around which the state politics has been entangled for the last several decades. After attaining Independence, the politics of who gets what, when, and how came to occupy a position of predominance. Politics highly charged with the expression of subnational identities does not remain normal as long as the animosity caused by the harsh fact of competitive ethnic pluralism continues to generate tension among different ethnic groups. As the assertion of the Assamese subnationalism became vocal and politically overbearing, the others were reminded of their own distinctive sociocultural identity. As a result, they too began to assert themselves politically by demanding the creation of a distinct homeland for themselves.

The other aspect of the situation concerns the presence of the illegal migrants who, for all practical purposes, evoke in the Assamese mind the fear that the Assamese people are at a double jeopardy. If, on the one hand, they confront the possibility of being weighed down and reduced to a minority in their own land, they also, on the other hand, feel that they are likely to lose economically to the rapacious outsiders. This deeply ingrained feeling of being colonized is one of the most influential factors that lends a particular colour to politics in Assam (Roy, Miri and Goswami 2007).

The politics of the state in the post-Independence period revolved around two major issues, namely language and land. The communal trouble, the integration of the princely states and the difficulties of organizing the various subnationalities into a single constitutional State structure were some of the problems that confronted the Indian state after attaining Independence. The Indian National Congress (INC) while directing all its efforts towards negotiating the transfer of power, a process in which it gave low priority to various conflicting interests of economic, political and linguistic[1] nature, only kept in suspension the resolution of the problems. They pointed out the difficulties involved in achieving them within the colonial structure but agreed to take up these issues and resolve them after the transfer of power. Independence in 1947 thus became a signal for agitation favouring realignment of state boundaries on linguistic basis (Goswami 1997). The partition of the country into two separate states did not, in any way, facilitate the solution of the language problem either in India or Pakistan. If anything, Partition further complicated the language question and brought in its wake a complex web of new problems. For instance, it brought in the most baffling refugee problem.

Historical reasons apart, as a result of India's Independence and Partition, Assam lost its Muslim- and Bengali-dominated Sylhet district to East Pakistan, but predominantly Bengali-speaking Cachar district remained with Assam. This provided, as it historically did in most part of India, a specific area for political manipulation (Goswami 1997).

---

[1] The Congress party conceded to the demand of Swarastra by Andhre in Madras Presidency in its annual session in 1938. For details, refer to Das (1970).

The Partition also brought into its wake the problem of Hindu refugees in the state. During the post-Independence period of 1951–1961, the migration process had suddenly picked up and the problem became more acute, contrary to the general expectations that the Partition would put an end to the influx of migrants from the newly emerged East Pakistan. Pakyntein thus remarked, 'even setting up of the two dominions of India and Pakistan did not prove a deterrent to these settlers who continued to pour in even after partition' (Census Report of Assam, 1961). The sentiment of the Assamese middle class in the wake of the continuous inflow of refugees is well reflected in the editorial of *The Assam Tribune* on refugees, which ran as follows:

> Since independence, the attack is being carried on from two flanks. First, there are the Muslim immigrants whose love and attachment to Pakistan are as strong as ever. There is no evidence of a change of heart and yet they find it much easier to migrate to this province under the shelter of the secular state policy of the Government of India. Then, there are the Hindu immigrants who apparently want to create a Bengal in this province. (*The Assam Tribune*, 18 July 1949, cited in Goswami 1997:27)

The Government of India (GoI) seemed not to be particularly concerned about it. For this reason, the *paper further* cautioned, 'The Centre must not be blind to Assam interest and must not adopt any policy that will ultimately lead to the annihilation of Assam. The danger point had almost been reached, and the Centre expects Assam to commit suicide with her eyes wide open' (*The Assam Tribune*, 18 July 1949, cited in Goswami 1997:27). A section of the conscious Assamese middle class of this period raised their voice by publishing letters to the editor,[2] for a timely solution of the refugee problem. Probably in view of such pleas from the Assamese middle class, the Indian parliament passed the Immigrants (Expulsion from Assam) Act in February 1950. The migration process had suddenly picked up during the period from 1951 to 1961. The failure to effectively control the influx of immigrants from East Pakistan, subsequently Bangladesh, has

[2] 'The refugee problem being an all-India problem, these peoples should be distributed equitably among all the states in the Indian union' (*The Assam Tribune*).

added a new dimension to Assam's demographic balance. The influx of refugees from East Bengal into Assam made the Assamese ruling class apprehensive of the new entrants into the state as they might one day outbalance the Assamese people leading to eventual loss of their newly acquired political status. This apprehension coupled with the economic effects of migration of refugees in thousands resulted in periodic upheavals and social conflict in the state. In the early part of February–March 1950, communal feelings were worked up to an unprecedented height. The constant flow of immigrants, food security, natural disasters, poverty and inadequate economic and industrial growth have further generated serious problems for the government. As the first chief minister of the state, Gopinath Bordoloi had therefore faced several challenges immediately after Independence. At a stage when a state should have been receiving grants from the Centre for the development of the state, even proposed grant for reconstruction programme was reduced, thereby creating stagnation in the growth of the state economy (e.g., an expected grant of ₹8 crore was reduced to ₹1.60 lakhs in the year 1949).[3] Realizing that the gravity of the situation had resulted from the unfettered flow of immigration, Sri Prakash, the then governor of Assam, thus expressed himself:

> Immigration from Eastern Bengal to Assam has already created various social and economic problems, and succeeding governments of the province have tackled it, encouraged or discouraged it as it moved their fancy or conformed to their wishes. With the definite separation of these two contiguous territories as parts of different independent dominions, the problem has assumed an altogether new aspect getting complicated as was inevitable with political considerations, and has got naturally and unavoidably to be met in a different way.[4]

Thus, Partition had added a new dimension to the Assamese society. In a memorandum[5] addressed to Sri Prakash, the then Minister of Scientific Research and Natural Resources, GoI, and President of

[3] Budget speech of Bishnuram Medhi, Finance Minister of Assam, 10 March 1949.

[4] *Assam Gazette*, Part VI, 15 March 1950.

[5] Memorandum submitted by the Asom Jatiya Mahasabha to the honourable Sri Prakash, Minister of Scientific Research and Natural Resources, Government of India,

Assam Refugee Rehabilitation Enquiry Committee, the Asom Jatiya Mahasabha expressed its concern in the following manner:

> The problem of Bengali refugees in Assam definitely means a vision of the creation of Brihattar Banga Samrajya, based on Bengalism of Bengali language, in which combined efforts of a powerful section of Bengali speaking old settlers of Assam, West Bengal, East Pakistan and also of the Bengali settlers in others parts of India, who think of themselves more in terms of Bengali than Indian, can easily be seen from the trend of their mentality and movements. Behind this Bengali refugee relief movement as carried on by the Bengalis, and their persistent effort to rehabilitate them in Assam beyond her capacity, lies this motive aimed at disruption of the strength of the Indian union for a sovereign Bengal. (Goswami 1997, 28)

It may, however, be noted that the Assamese leadership was opposed to the entry of Bengali refugees only. For instance, the Jatiya Mahasabha expressed a preference for refugees from Punjab rather than Bengal. In a similar tune, *The Assam Tribune*, the leading newspaper of the state, in one of its editorials also pleaded that Assam should welcome a quota of refugees from Punjab. The Assamese middle class apprehended that since the Bengali population had already constituted a sizeable section in the state, the new Bengali refugees would strengthen the cause of the Bengalis, posing a severe threat to Assamese language and culture. In view of this, the local press in Assam criticized the policy of the central government regarding the refugee problem and asked, 'Had Assam no right to exist as the land of Assamese people? Is it the intention of the government to turn the Assamese people into minority community in their own province and jeopardize their language, culture and their very existence?' (*The Assam Tribune*).

On the other hand, the then Prime Minister Nehru wrote to Bordoloi in one of his letters: 'There is no bar to individuals coming, but I think you would be justified in stopping large groups from coming, unless they come with approval.'[6] On another occasion, when

and President, Assam Refugee Rehabilitation Enquiry Committee, Camp Guwahati, 4 July 1951.

[6] Nehru to Bordoloi, 15 March 1948, Assam Secretariat Files, cited by Barooah (2010, 332).

Bordoloi's government stated that there was not even sufficient land to provide to the local landless people, Nehru commented, 'If Assam adopts an attitude of incapacity to help in solving the refugee problem, then the claims of Assam for financial help obviously suffer.'[7] Nehru also added further that if land was not available in Assam, then it was wrong to expect that it would still be available in any other parts of the country.[8] In another instance, the prime minister said that he was definitely opposed to mass exchange of populations, but on the other hand, he insisted that all those people who expressed wish to cross the border in either directions had to be allowed to do so in order to erase the fears of minorities. Thus, it cannot be denied that Nehru was not concerned about the issue of unabated influx into Assam. Although the issue was aptly raised in the assembly and Bordoloi had repeatedly requested for help from the Centre to bail Assam out of the extraordinarily difficult situation, the Congress party could not argue with a firm and consolidated hand for its cause in front of the Centre, which contributed to continuation of the problem in the subsequent years. It is true that expelling immigrants from Assam was the greater responsibility of the Centre. But Bordoloi's appeal for devolution of power to the state remained unheard.[9] 'The seeds of separatism', writes Misra, 'which would overtake the state in the years to follow, lay embedded in the policies and prejudices of the central Congress leadership towards Assam' (*The Assam Tribune*).

This problem was, however, finally recognized by the central government in 1950 when Parliament passed the Immigrants (Expulsion from Assam) Act, 1950. But the Act lacked proper machinery and the procedure followed for expulsion did not garner much support from the Centre. Besides, the Centre's direction as regards granting political rights to refugees from Pakistan is quite relaxed. A simple declaration of his/her refugee status is sufficient for attaining political rights. The

---

[7] Nehru to Bordoloi, 18 May 1949, cited by Barooah (2010, 394).

[8] Nehru to Bordoloi, 18 May 1949, cited by Barooah (2010, 394).

[9] Although the Assamese elite were strongly in favour of state autonomy, yet their pleas went unheard as this voice was unorganized. Most of the central leaders wanted a federation with a strong centre. Hence, devolution of power was unacceptable to them.

Act remained, for all practical purposes, a dead letter and subsequently went into disuse by 1957. Immigration continued without any barrier and politics of the state has been deeply influenced by the influx of people from Bangladesh. Interestingly, however, immigration issue was not a major subject of political controversy during the periods after Independence till the Assam movement that started in 1979. Since Independence the ethnic Assamese political leadership, in response to popular campaigns, pursued cultural policies that sought to assert a truly Assamese identity for the state; for instance, to have Assamese as the official language of the state and as the language of instruction in the state's educational institutions. In a sense, post Independence, an attempt at Assamization of position and power appeared to gain ground howsoever imperceptibly. The political leadership of the Bengali Muslim community insulated the influx issue from language issue that dominated the scene, by getting that community to declare Assamese as their mother tongue in the census enumerations. The language controversy was incidentally a conflict between the Assamese and Bengali Hindu communities. The political parties dependent on support across the communities agreed not to raise this inconvenient influx issue. But they hardly contributed to a genuine integration of communities and the evolution of a composite cultural pattern (Goswami 1997). In this context, Sanjib Baruah (1986) remarked:

> Two factors that helped to keep the immigration issue out of the political agenda were the centrality of the language issue in defining the contours of ethnic conflict in the state and the aggregation of interest within political parties, primarily in the Congress, but in other parties as well, which in effect produced a tacit agreement not to raise this explosive issue.

In fact, the immigration issue was one of the main props of the long Congress rule in the state. The electoral statistics for the period 1957–1979 clearly indicate the significant increase in the number of voters during this period (Goswami 1995).

THE STATE LANGUAGE ISSUE

The change in the power structure in Assam in the wake of indepen-dence had given Assamese leaders political leverage for controlling the ethnic division of labour which in turn stimulated competition and conflict. Consequently, governmental authority was directed towards restructuring the ethnic division of labour, which in turn had intensified the conflict between the Assamese and Bengali Hindus. For example, in the riots of 1948 and 1950 the starting point was the demand by Assamese youth on the Bengalis to shed the sign of separatism, namely to replace Bengali shop signboards with Assamese, to desist from running separate schools for Bengalis and finally to accept Assamese as their language.[10] The Calcutta Press, however, termed this agitation 'Bengali Kheda' (Drive away Bengalis) movement (Goswami 1997, 34). In 1948 there was a demand for a separate Bengali-dominated independent state with the districts of Cachar, Karimganj, Lushai Hills and Tripura. Satindra Mohan Das took the lead in this move. Thus, the language issue assumed a great political importance immediately after Independence, and the language policy in Assam became the bone of contention between the Assamese and Bengali communities.

Meanwhile the Assam Government Education Department had issued a circular to all Inspectors and Deputy Inspectors of Schools directing them to take steps for making Assamese the compulsory medium of instruction in all schools of Assam valley. In places where the spoken language was used as medium for the primary education, Assamese was taught as the second language. Assamese language was to replace Bengali in course of time in all those schools where Bengali was the sole medium of instruction. Bengali Muslims and Migrant labourers were generally provided admission in the Assamese schools. But the Bengali Hindus continued to insist that their schools should have the Bengali medium. There was strong resentment (*Hindustan Standard*, 5 July 1955) from the Bengali middle class in Assam against this policy of the government and they voiced their demands through an organization called Cachar District Committee. Another association known as Assam–Bengal Association echoed a similar sentiment when

[10] Confidential Report of Enquiry into Goalpara Disturbance, April 1955.

it said that 'Bengalis were in majority in Assam and it would not take long to have Bengali as an accepted state language of Assam.'[11]

At this juncture, the Governor of Assam, Akbar Hydri, made the following statement[12] in the assembly which further complicated the issue:

> The natives of Assam are now masters of their own houses. They have a government which is both responsible and responsive to them. They can take what steps are necessary for the encouragement and propagation of Assamese language and culture and customs of tribal people, who are their fellow citizens and who also must have a share in the formulation of such policies. The Bengalis have no longer the power even if they had the will to impose anything on the people of the hills and valleys which constitutes Assam. The basis of such feeling against them; as exists fear but now there is no cause for fear. I would, therefore, appeal to you to exert all the influence you possess to give the stranger in our midst a fair deal, provided of course, he in his turn deals loyally with us.

All these developments became a matter of deep concern for the Bengali organizations in Assam. They approached Sardar Patel to dissuade the government of Assam from trying to impose Assamese language in their schools and also provide employment facilities to the employees hailing from Sylhet.[13] It was clear from their memorandum that the economic interest seemed to be the main issue, because they complained of the refusal on the part of the government to issue contract and trade licenses and permits to the Bengalis. However, the intervention from the central government seemed to have subsided the issue for something by asking the Assam government to induct Bengalis as well into administrative jobs (Das 1971, 185–187).

Thus it appears that the official language question in Assam touched upon the issue of employment as well as cultural identity. Therefore,

[11] Natun Asamiya, 18 August 1947.

[12] Assam Assembly debates, 5 November 1947.

[13] Clearly a middle-class demand, for it should be noted that Assamese language was meant to be the second language in Bengali schools and the official language continued to be English.

it became the focal point of controversy between the Assamese and Bengali communities. The Bengalis favoured parity in status between the Assamese and Bengali languages in Assam because that would mean equality of opportunity in employment and political and social status. The Assamese, on their end, viewed such duality as a perpetuation of Bengali domination in both cultural and employment spheres. For the Assamese middle class, due to historical reasons, it was the Hindu Bengali who stood as an obstacle to economic development. Therefore, after Independence the Assamese middle class made a bid to acquire sizeable control over the apparatus of the state administration, and share in the state-sponsored development process. They wanted the lion's share not only of the government jobs, but also of the financial resources of the state government. They mobilized a strong cultural campaign with this end in view. But their late start and the fact that big business had already spread its network into the farthest hooks and corners of the country made their efforts in business and industry weak and ineffectual (Gohain 1982). In consequence, they clung all the more tenaciously to their control over the state administration. Myron Weiner observed in this context:

> What characterized the Assamese quest for a cultural identity was their midst; it is quite likely that the presence of large numbers of migrants from other states, especially from Bengal, sharpened the sense of Assamese identity and gave it what many outsiders perceived as its peculiarly aggressive character. (Weiner 1978, 112–113)

The raising of the official language and medium of instruction issues brought linguistic chauvinism into the forefront. It is a sophisticated device of the ruling class to completely formalize education in the name of modernity and progressivism in order to perpetuate elitism. The sophistication lies in the linking of these issues with the question of the cultural and linguistic identity of various nationalities in our country. 'Chauvinism is one of the ideological tools which enables the bourgeoisie to maintain its domination over the proletariat' (Lowy 1976).

The development of regional movements in independent India, identified with regional language and tradition, obscured the fact that, within most of the states in India, there were serious divisions. There has been, first of all, the problem of forming the present state boundaries out of separate administrative units. Another problem involved the relationship of minority groups to the major section of the population of the state. Weiner (1978) observed that there are at least two special types of minorities: (a) linguistic minorities belonging to linguistic groups which are majorities elsewhere and (b) minorities which are not majorities elsewhere. The minority group presses for the preservation of its language in schools and may demand that administrative ordinances be published in its own language. If the particular minority groups claim functional recognition to be a majority language of a neighbouring state and if the size of this minority is substantial, it raises difficult political problems of interethnic rivalry including violence.

The Congress championed the cause of the 'Asomiya national identity' in terms of safeguarding Assamese language and culture at the initial period after Independence. The election appeal of the Assam Pradesh Congress party reveals:

> Unless the province of Assam be organized on the basis of the Assamese language and Assamese culture, the survival of the Assamese nationality and culture will become impossible. The inclusion of Bengali-speaking Sylhet and Cacher (plains portion) and the immigration or importation of lacs of Bengali settlers on the wastelands has been threatening to destroy the distinctness of Assam and has, in practice, caused many disorders in its administration. For an appropriate solution of this problem, the Congress party be installed as the majority party in the assembly. (Guha 1977)

But the Congress party was forced to redefine its support base as in the aftermath of independence and partition, the predominantly Bengali-speaking district of Cachar has remained with Assam making Bengali Hindus and Muslims electorally significant. During the first three decades of the 'Congress dominance system', the party drew its support from a wider social base that included caste Hindu Assamese, Bengali Hindus and Muslims, tea tribes and other linguistic minorities. The Congress barely lost 3–4 seats out of 12 or 14 constituencies in the first six general elections as well in assembly elections the party had highest number of seats. Even when voters in other parts of India had overwhelmingly rejected the Congress party of Indira Gandhi as a result of the emergency in 1977, Assam returned 10 out of 14 seats to the party with a vote share of 50.6 per cent (Goswami 2003, 224). At the same time, the diverse demographic mix of the state made Congress's 'catch-all' support base a fragile one. But since 1978 scenario has drastically changed (Tables 2.1 and 2.2).

Table 2.1 *Lok Sabha Elections: 1952–1985*

			INC	
Year	Total Seats	Turn Out	Seats	Vote
1952	12	47.7	11	45.7
1957	12	46.6	9	51.7
1962	12	52.8	9	45.2
1967	14	59.3	10	45.8
1971	14	50.7	13	57.0
1977	14	54.9	10	50.6
1980	14[a]	53.4	2	51.0
1984	14	79.7	4	23.6

Note: Remaining seats and votes have gone to other parties or independents.

[a] Election was held only for two Lok Sabha seats in 1980.

Table 2.2 *Assembly Elections: 1952–1983*

			INC	
	Total Seat	Vote Share	Seats Won	Vote Share
1952	108	61.1	75	43.5
1957	108	58.6	71	52.4
1962	105	52.8	79	48.3
1967	126	61.3	73	43.6
1972	114	61.7	94	53.2
1978	126	66.9	8	8.8
1983	126	32.7	91	52.5

Note: Remaining seats and votes have gone to other parties or independents.

However, with the continuous influx of refugees from the erstwhile East Pakistan and with more and more tribal communities such as the Khasis, Garos and Bodos starting to assert their own identities, the situation became more complex. The Asomiya middle class in the meantime became more assertive. With the policies pursued by the Congress on issues such as official language, medium of instruction and the establishment of refineries, the Assam Pradesh Congress had tried to do some tight rope walking. But the central leadership of the party appeared to be insensitive to the problems of the state. This insensitivity had become more and more pronounced slowly. The Congress's attitudes towards the demands of the various groups like the hill tribes and the Bodos showed elements of uncertainty. For instance, when the Bodos demanded introduction of Bodo as a medium of instruction up to the secondary level in the then Goalpara district in 1968, the then chief minister stated it to be contradictory to the government educational policy. The demand of a separate state made by the hill tribes like the Khasis, Jaintiyas and Garos, which was articulated by the All Party Hill Leaders Conference (APHLC), too did not receive a sympathetic response in the beginning. In fact, the APHLC legislators resigned en bloc from the Assam Assembly, soon after the 1967 assembly elections, in order to pressurize the central government for the formation of a separate hill state. It is true that on the eve of elections the Congress always took steps to gain popularity and tried to undo the damages caused by its policies. Till the late 1960s and early 1970s the Asomiya middle class seemed to have influenced the affairs of the state through the Congress party. But tussle for leadership within the Congress party had led to the emergence of factional politics which contributed to the erosion of its support base. It is interesting to note that when the Congress party had started losing its original support base for the reasons discussed above, some regional political groups and parties had also emerged in Assam. For example, the APHLC with its non-Assamese-speaking ethnic support base began to improve its position in the state. But the regional groups formed in the Asomiya-dominated areas like the People's Democratic Party and the Ujani Asom Rajya Parishad (UARP) could not make any mark in the electoral politics of the state. It was only after the six-year long Assam Movement that the regional forces could become a significant force in the electoral field. It was under such circumstances that the compulsions of parliamentary politics seemed to have forced the Congress to concentrate more on the most organized and insecure sections of the society in Assam, namely the tea garden and the immigrant populations. The rural Muslims and the tea labourer voters had a tendency of voting en bloc for the Congress (Deka 1976). Assam has a large tea garden labour population and the Indian National Trade Union Congress (INTUC) could penetrate within this section of the communities. The Muslim immigrants for being insecure have become more and more relevant in electoral terms as their numbers have increased substantively over the years. Besides, owing to the continuous influx of refugees from the erstwhile East Pakistan and more and more tribal communities like the Khasis, Garos and Bodos having begun to assert their own identities, the situation became increasingly complicated. Besides, the Asomiya middle class had become more aggressive. It was evident from the policies pursued by the Congress on issues such as official language, medium of instruction and establishment of refineries that the Assam Pradesh Congress had tried to take some uncertain moves. For instance, on the issue of the establishment of a second oil refinery in Assam and the demand of a separate hill state, the Assam Congress took courses of action which actually alienated the large sections of the population who were supporting these demands, and then it tried to salvage the situation by announcing measures to placate these sections just before the elections (Narain 1976).

CHANGE OF GOVERNMENT IN THE STATE

The change of government in the Centre led to corresponding changes in the political alignment in the state. Although the same issue of Emergency excesses remained central to the campaigns of both the 1977 parliamentary and 1978 assembly elections, the results were very different. To resist the Congress, the Opposition parties had joined hands to form the Janata Party (JP) in February 1977 but could not make much of a dent in the general elections in the state unlike that in the rest of India. In the 1977 elections, the Congress bagged 10 of the 14 seats (Table 2.1), while the JP could pocket only 3 (Guwahati, Tezpur and Mangaldoi). Besides, Charan Narzari from Plain Tribes Council of Assam (PTCA) supported by the JP could wrest the Kokrajhar seat from the Congress. Apart from PTCA, UARP was a Janata ally then. The first major setback for the Congress in the state came during 1978 assembly elections. The Congress could win only 8 seats and polled 23.7 per cent of the valid votes. But these elections were held after the JP's ascent to power at the Centre. The change of government at the Centre, leading to corresponding changes in the political alignment in the state, had affected the results of these elections. With the defeat of Congress party, the very foundation of the state Congress was shaken. A non-Congress government came to power in the state under the leadership of Golap Borbora of the JP. The JP in the state included ex-Congressmen (particularly of high castes), the members of Jana Sangh (JS), the Swatantra Party and the Socialist Party. Besides these national parties, two other regional parties—the People's Democratic Party of Assam (PDPA) and the UARP—also merged with the JP. Except for the Socialist Party, all the other parties neither had any significant following nor any good organizational set-up. Therefore, the ex-socialists became the most dominant faction within the Janata. The PTCA became an electoral partner of the JP. The installation of Janata-led government could hardly instil political stability and legitimacy as factionalism and intraparty conflict toppled the government. The JP in the state like the one at the Centre remained inherently unstable because it was a coalition of disparate political sections. The state was plunged into a major crisis as evident from a series of three changes of the government within a short span of time. The Janata-led government in Assam collapsed within 20 months in November 1979. Simply speaking, the Janata experiment also failed to meet the popular expectations. This shows the limitation of the alternative party to the Congress idea both at the Centre and the state. (Hussain 1993, 98) The Janata government failed in Assam even before the 1980 Lok Sabha elections, giving way to a short-lived Congress ministry. By that time the Assam Movement had already hit its peak.

This chapter has presented the major issues around which the state politics has been entangled since independence. In the next chapter, we explore the causes that led to the Assam Movement.

REFERENCES

Barooah, Nirode K. 2010. *Gopinath Bordoloi, 'The Assam Problem' and Nehru's Centre*. Guwahati: Bhabani Print and Publications.

Baruah, Sanjib. 1986. 'Lessons of Assam'. *Economic & Political Weekly* 21 (7, 15 February): 232–284.

Das, D. 1970. *From Curzon to Nehru and After*. New York, NY: John Day.

———, ed. 1971. *Sardar Patel's Correspondence 1945–50*. Vol. 9. Ahmedabad: Navajivan Press.

Deka, K. N. 1976. 'Assam'. In *State Politics in India*, edited by Iqbal Narain, 30–50. Meerut: Meenakshi Prakashan.

Gohain, H. 1982. 'Ethnic Conflict in Assam in Thakur'. In *India's North East: A Multifaceted View*, edited by P. Thakur, 165. Tinsukia: Prakash Publishing House.

Goswami, Sandhya. 1995. 'Population Migration and Its Impact on Assam's Economic and Social Milieu'. *Journal of Political Science*.

———. 1997. *Language Politics in Assam*. New Delhi: Ajanta Publications.

———. 2003. 'Assam: Multiple Realignment and Fragmentation of Part System'. *Journal of Indian School of Political Economy* 15 (1–2, January–June): 221–247.

Guha, Amalendu. 1977. *Planter Raj to Swaraj: Freedom Struggle and Electoral Politics in Assam 1826–1947*. New Delhi: People's Publishing House.

Hussain, Monirul. 1993. *The Assam Movement: Class, Ideology and Identity*. New Delhi: Manak Publications.

Lowy, M. 1976. 'Marxism and the National Question'. *New Left Review* 96 (March–April): 81–100.

Medhi, Bishnuram. 1949. 'Budget Speech as Finance Minister of Assam, 10 March 1949'. *ALAD* 1 (1): 15.

Narain, Iqbal. 1976. *State Politics in India*. Meerut: Meenakshi Prakashan.

Roy, Ramashray, Sujata Miri, and Sandhya Goswami. 2007. *Northeast India: Development, Communalism and Insurgency*. Delhi: Anshah Publishing House, 27–50.

Weiner, M. 1978. *Sons of the Soil: Migration and Ethnic Conflict in India*. Princeton, NJ: Princeton University Press.

Assam Movement and Its Fallout

The Assam Movement was primarily aimed at ensuring the very distinct sociocultural, economic and political identity of the Assamese people in the face of a massive influx of immigrants from Bangladesh. The basic Assamese fear was that of losing their land. This was a much more basic issue than the identity question, because it called into question one of the defining characteristics of nationality, that is, territory and the loss of territory to people who settle on it tends to be permanent. This is a problem that distinguishes the Assam situation from that of any other part of India (Omvedt 1980). The right of every nationality to have equality of opportunity, economic growth and cultural development is a democratic one. The central issue raised by the movement's leaders was that of foreigners overswamping Assam and the need for a national response to this problem. Besides, the movement opposed the participation of foreign nationals in the electoral process of the state.

No social movement can emerge from a void. The Assam Movement too has a historical basis like all other social movements. It took a long time to take the shape of a distinctly visible social movement in November 1979, when the issue of illegal immigration became a serious concern in the political agenda of the state. The issue that was dormant for four decades returned to the fore of public agenda with a vengeance. The six-year long Assam Movement (1979–1985) was led by the All Assam Students' Union (AASU) in league with All Assam Gana Sangram Parishad (AAGSP). Although movement came to be known as the anti-foreigner movement, it cannot be ignored that it started as a movement against the *bahiragota* (outsiders) in the beginning.

Even though the Assam movement is known for its primary and most frequently stated aim—the expulsion of illegal nationals—it began with a plan of action that looked at comprehensive economic development for Assam through land reform measures; industrialization; nationalization of private industries; stopping the eviction of poor peasants from the reserved forest areas of Dayang, Kaki and Mingmon; the control of floods; and government intervention in the procurement and distribution of food grains. It was, however, the emotive issue of cultural and racial identity, disseminated among the people through the AASU's quite incomparable spread and influence, that began to dominate the movement from the start. This is also the predominant memory that remains of the movement today (Dutta 2012, 60).

The Assamese middle class, mainly students, teachers and lawyers played the leading role in the movement. The deep disillusionment of the Assamese people with the Indian State for its continued neglect towards the structural issues that had been confronting the state since Independence seemed to have contributed to mobilize a large section of the Assamese people against the State. Its success was further ensured due to the strong support it received from the rural masses.

> Mass participation and popular backing made the Assam movement historically as well as sociologically very significant among the well-known social movements that India has experienced during the postcolonial period. Though there are examples of historically significant movement like the Telengana movement of the early fifties, the Naxalbari movement based on Maoist ideology of rural insurrection of the late sixties. But admittedly, all those movements stand nowhere near the Assam Movement in terms of mass mobilization and participation. (Hussain 1993)

The zeal and passion for the cause that were witnessed during the Assam Movement had also been accompanied by a rage of increasing intolerance towards dissent and criticism. Despite non-violence being an enshrined principle of the movement, violence did erupt on several occasions. The leadership of the movement failed to contain the anti-democratic, non-secular and violent tendencies generated by the movement itself. Hiren Gohain thus writes, 'Several leaders of AASU and the Assam Jatiyatabadi Dal have made incendiary speeches inciting violence against leftists as traitors. A particularly revealing side-light has been the decisive anti-left orientation of the move-ment.' The chauvinistic undertones of the movement had no doubt influenced the social fabrics of the state (Gohain 1980, 18–19). The feeling of apprehension of a severe threat to the Assamese identity—politically, culturally and economically—appeared when it was found that a large number of foreign nationals were enlisted in the voters' list of the Mangaldoi Lok Sabha constituency where a by-election was to be held in May 1979. Recognizing the seriousness of the problem, the then Chief Election Commissioner of India, in charge of conducting free and fair elections, himself expressed on 24 October 1978:

> I would like to refer to the alarming situation in some states, especially in the North eastern region, wherefrom reports are coming regarding large scale inclusion of foreign nationals in the electoral rolls; in one case, the population in 1971 census recorded an increase as high as 34.98 per cent over 1961 census figures and this figure was attributed to the influx of large number of persons from foreign countries. The influx has become a regular feature. I think it may not be a wrong assessment to make that on the basis of increase of 34.98 per cent between two census, the increase would likely to be recorded in the 1991 census would be more than 100 per cent over 1961 census. In other words, a stage would be reached when that state may have to reckon with the foreign nationals who may be in all probability constitute a sizeable percentage if not the majority of population in the state. (Hussain 1993, 102)

This statement sparked off the Assam Movement that continued to rock the state till 1985 (Baruah 1986).

In reality, the movement began during the last days of Janata government in the state. In the 1978 Assam Assembly elections, Congress was voted out of power in the state. The JP alliance formed the first ever non-Congress government in Assam. However, from the very beginning, Janata government was unstable because of internal conflicts and contradictions within the parties that supported the government. The Janata ministry headed by Golap Borbora collapsed in September 1979. A coalition ministry headed by Jogen Hazarika with the faction of erstwhile Janata party, failed within three months. Emergency was imposed in 1979 and was force for a year. The Congress (I) returned to power at the Centre under Indira Gandhi in the early 1980 elections. After Mrs Gandhi assumed office in Delhi, massive defection took place in the politics of Assam. Congress (I), which won only eight seats in the 1978 elections, increased the strength of its MLAs to 45 in December 1980 as a consequence of defections. However the party failed to reach the majority number in the assembly. At this point of time, under the patronage of Mrs Gandhi, Congress (I) formed a government in Assam on 6 December 1980 with Mrs Anuwara Taimur as the chief minister, which lasted till 26 June 1981. Taimur's elevation as the chief minister of Assam, at this point of time, turned the Assam Movement into a communal playground. The AASU strongly opposed the formation of Taimur-led government in the state and it successfully observed total *bandhs* in the state to register its protest on the day Taimur's government assumed office (Hussain 1993, 147). A section of vernacular press began to spread the news that the new government would encourage Muslim immigration further and they would be benefited in getting the government jobs and other services under the Muslim chief minister. As a reaction to the Muslim threat created by the press, the influence of RSS and BJP on Assam Movement suddenly increased (Hussain 1993, 301). Taimur government on its part created a kind of legitimacy crisis in the state by aiming at de-Assamization of state bureaucracy (Baruah 1999, 129). Anuwara Taimur's selection as the chief minister of Assam by the Congress High Command was considered not democratic at that stage. Earlier, Muslim Congress stalwarts like Fakharuddin Ali Ahmed and Moinul Hoque Chowdhury were never considered for the post of chief minister of Assam by Congress High Command. Besides, Taimur was not a very prominent and mass-based leader. She did not even demand for chief ministership. Nevertheless, the Congress made her chief minister of Assam only to create a Muslim vote bank in favour of the party. Mrs Gandhi realized that the Muslims of Assam were in crisis because of the Assam Movement and if Congress could show its sympathy towards them at that point of time, the community would be a vote bank for the party. Such a divisive strategy of the Congress party has no doubt given its dividend in the 1983 Assam Assembly elections when the immigrant Muslim community solidly backed the party against the movement.

ELECTION 1983

The sixth Assam Legislative Assembly was dissolved prematurely on 19 March 1982. The government was determined to hold assembly elections in the state by March 1983. The state was definite that an election with a moderate or high turnout would weaken the claims of the movement leaders. On the other hand, the leadership of the movement was also equally adamant not to support the election without the removal of the names of illegal immigrants from the electoral rolls. The organizers of the movement called for a boycott of the election, portraying it as Assam's 'last struggle for survival'. Not only the leaders but even the opinions of various organizations over boycotting or participating in the elections were sharply divided. The 1983 elections thus became the focus of a contest between the Assam Movement and the Indian State (Baruah 1999, 131). The boycott call given by the movement leaders was highly successful specially in the constituencies dominated by 'indigenous' Assamese population, where voter turnout had come down to as low as 0.38 per cent, 0.40 per cent and 0.68 per cent. The average voting percentage was, however, 31.46 per cent. It was due to the fact that hill districts, Barak Valley and immigrant dominant constituencies were not affected by the poll boy-cott call. Besides, in 17 constituencies elections had to be cancelled for the total breakdown of law and order situation. The immigrants, both Muslims and Hindus, rallied behind the Congress in this election. As a consequence, the Congress party could win 91 seats out of the total 109, where elections were held. The total number of Muslim candidates elected was 33, out of which 26 candidates were from Congress. Prime Minister Indira Gandhi campaigned for three consecutive days and addressed election meetings only in the immigrant-inhabited areas in the Barak Valley and Brahmaputra Valley. Even two central ministers, namely A. B. A. Gani Khan Choudhury and Nihar Ranjan Laskar, also campaigned in minority-dominated areas. The Congress leaders appealed to the Bengali Hindus and immigrant Muslims to rally behind the Congress and oppose the Assam Movement. Both the central ministers made highly communal statements during the election campaign in minority-dominated areas (Nath 2015, 134). On the other hand, BJP leaders like Atal Behari Vajpayee campaigned against the election. The vernacular press, during the election, overwhelmingly supported every move of the movement leaders and labelled every minority who participated in the election as illegal Bangladeshis.

The election of 1983 was a political disaster as the Congress came to power without any popular mandate. The state imposed different black laws like Assam Special Power (Press) Act which censored the media and imposed Essential Services Maintenance Act (ESMA) on state government employees to ensure their participation in the process of the election. Most of the top leaders of the movement were arrested and and send them to jail for obstruction of holding the election. The state experienced unprecedented breakdown of law and order and violence during this election. The AASU declared that as many as 130 supporters of the movement were martyred in government violence during the election. On the other hand, government declared that 3,026 persons lost their lives in election-related violence. The Report of the Commission of Enquiry on Assam Disturbance, 1983, recorded that during the period from 1 January and 30 April 1983, in election-related violence, the loss of lives in different districts were: Dibrugarh 54, Sivasagar 88, Lakhimpur 350, Nagaon 1,811, Karbi Anglong 16, Darrang 493, Kamrup 92 and Goalpara 119 (Nath 2015, 135). At different places, Assam Movement supporters used force and involved in violence in order to pressurizing the government not to hold the election. These incidents of election-related violence eroded the non-violent character of Assam Movement. During the elections, communal clashes occurred at different places in the state. The election was held in three phases on 14, 17 and 20 February 1983. In the second phase of election, 500 immigrant Muslims and same number of Hindu Bengalis were killed in communal clashes in Saolkhowa, south of Mangaldoi, and in Khairabari, north of Mangaldoi. Several villages were burnt during the period of 10–12 February, in Gahpur of Sonitpur district where at least 150 people died and 2,500 became homeless (Borpujari 1999, 52). On 18 February 1983, a large-scale massacre took place in Nellie, near Jagiroad of Nagaon district, where around 1,600 people died. In this incident, the local people, including the Assamese and tribes, attacked the Muslim immigrants from East Bengal (Kimura 2003, 227). Meanwhile, the central government's decision to conduct elections despite the boycott call given by the leaders of the movement in 1983 led to massive carnages. Nellie, Gohpur, Silapathar, Chamaria and Dhula became well known, for such heinous massacre.

The Nellie massacre was one of the most gruesome massacres in independent India. Election was a factor for this massacre. The Congress's largest blunder was imposing the election on an already tense and divided society. Without the election, the killings and associated carnage would not have happened. The movement leaders declined having any role in the massacre and put the blame on the local Tiwa tribe living nearby areas of Nellie. However, it was clear that the massacre was a revenge on the immigrant Muslims living in that area for their participation in the election. On 10 April 1983, newly elected Chief Minister Hiteswar Saikia alleged that the volunteer force of AASU led the Nellie massacre (Nath 2015, 207). The 1983 Assam Assembly election and the Nellie massacre sharply divided the movement on communal lines, and also visibly established the enemies for both the supporters and opponents of the movement. The election made the immigrant Muslims 'enemy' for the movement supporters, whereas Nellie massacre posited the movement supporters as the 'enemy' for the immigrant Muslims. Even a section of indigenous Muslims, who supported the movement from its beginning, began to rethink about their position in view of the growing anti-Muslim sentiment of the movement that became visible in Nellie.

The government led by Hiteswar Saikia that came to power lacked both legitimacy and credibility. The farcical nature of this election was a matter of record set out in the report of the state's chief electoral officer and even in other documents of the Election Commission. However, in spite of all efforts, elections could not be held in 7 of the 12 constituencies and a majority of the constituencies in the Brahmaputra Valley remained unrepresented throughout the life of the Seventh Lok Sabha. It was during this Lok Sabha period that the controversial Illegal Migrants (Determination by Tribunals) (IMDT) Act, 1983, was promulgated. However, while admitting the opportunism that went into the formulation of this Act, one also has to consider the political circumstances that made the Act necessary at that point of time (Prabhakara 2005).

The worst violence occurred in villages around Nellie, an area where the Tiwa people once had their kingdom. Most of the area is inhabited by Bengali immigrants and their descendants. Tiwas (also called Lalungs) are a 'plains tribe' community, who had lost much of their traditional land to these immigrants from East Bengal. Colonial administrators viewed them as 'Hinduized' tribes who were not isolated and 'backward' enough to need the kind of protection offered to the more 'backward' and isolated 'hill tribes'. The Line System that sought to protect the traditional land rights, which in the post-independence period took the form of policies restricting land transfer in 'tribal blocks', has generally been found to be far too weak to enable the tribes to defend their lands.

Although in the Nellie massacre the plain tribal Tiwas and the ethnic Assamese were on the same side, in another location of major violence, namely Gohpur, the Bodos and ethnic Assamese fought against each other. The PTCA, while contesting the elections, in those areas owing to the longstanding local dispute between Bodo and ethnic Assamese peasants over the occupation of land, got entangled in the election controversy. The land was government land, and part of the Gohpur reserve forest, which PTCA promised to return to the Bodo inhabitants. PTCA had also advocated a separate plains tribal state called Udayachal and parts of the Gohpur area, especially the reserve forests, that fall within the borders of the proposed separate state. Supporting PTCA was seen as an action for a dispensation that would bring back Bodos some of that land. The Gohpur violence, as Sekhar Gupta puts it, 'brought out in sharp relief the basic weaknesses and contradictions of Assamese society, and had a far-reaching impact on the course of the agitation later' (Baruah 1999, 134–135; Gupta 1984, 11–12).

The AASU formed a *seswasevak bahini* (volunteer force) in 1980 to mobilize the movement. And many believed that the force was formed at the behest of the RSS. The supreme commander of the *seswasevak bahini,* Joynath Sarma, who became minister under the Asom Gana

Parishad (AGP) government in 1985, was known to be very close to RSS (Nath 2015, 221). Many believe that the *bahini* was involved in several communal clashes that occurred during the movement (Nath 2015, 165). On 21 February 1982, RSS convened a *Purbanchaliya Hindu Sanmillan* in Guwahati, where all Hindus were appealed to unite under Hindu religious flag, irrespective of caste and language, so that they could play a dominant and determining role in the entire Northeast. Such appeal, in the midst of Assam Movement, worked as a catalyst to unite Hindus against the Muslims (Borgohain 2001, 15). The Akhil Bharatiya Vidyarthi Parishad (ABVP) strongly supported the cause of Assam Movement and it organized several seminars on the issue of the movement in different places such as Delhi, Hyderabad and Bhubaneswar. Even some prominent leaders of the movement joined the seminar held in Hyderabad. On the day of *Rakhi Bandhan* in 1983, ABVP used lakhs of *Assam Rakhi* throughout the country and observed the occasion as 'Save Assam Day'. A delegation of the organization carried a *Swahid Jyoti* (martyr light) from Rajghat and handed it over to the AASU leaders in Guwahati on 1 October 1983. Next day, ABVP organized a mass satyagraha in Guwahati in support of the movement where almost 1,000 members of the organization from all over the country participated.

The Assam Movement made 'Jamiat' very relevant among the Muslims of Assam against the idea that the movement was controlled by RSS. By the end of 1980, Jamiat began to advocate the cause of the minorities and took the lead to unite all the minority organizations against the movement. It even aligned with the Citizens' Right Preservation Committee (CRPC), which was an organization of Hindu Bengalis, the linguistic minority of Assam. It played an important role in creation of the All Assam Minority Students' Union (AAMSU) in 1980 as an opposition to the AASU and Assam Movement (Ahmed 1999, 149–151). During the movement, through regular publications, Jamiat tried to poison the minds of Muslim readers (Hussain 1993, 132) against the Assam Movement and the Hindus. Jamiat brought in religious leaders from different parts of India, during the entire movement period, to campaign against the movement in the immigrant Muslim-dominated areas with an objective to unite the

Muslims against the movement. Jamiat even termed the leaders of Assam Movement as 'extremist' and 'secessionist'. In a resolution of the Jamiat during the Assam unit's 14th conference, held on 24–25 April 1984, it said, 'due to abnormal situation arising out of the result of so called foreigners movement launched by the extremist secessionist force since the last 4/5 years constantly threatening the sense of security of the people belonging to all minority communities ...' (as cited in Ahmed 1999, 207).

A minority convention was held in Jaleswar in Goalpara district on 29–30 March 1980. Mainly Muslim politicians and youths and a section of Hindu Bengali leaders participated in the convention. In the convention, AAMSU and All Assam Minority Yuva Parishad (AAMYP) were formed to protect and safeguard the minority communities from the Assam Movement (Ahmed 1999, 150). Till the beginning of Assam movement, AASU was strongly supported by the students from immigrant Muslim community and the organization had strong presence in the educational institutions located at the areas inhabited by these Muslims. After the beginning of the Assam Movement, particularly after the formation of AAMSU, immigrant Muslims as a community deserted AASU. The community began to consider it as a threat and AAMSU emerged as the new platform of young leaders and students from the community. However, the indigenous Muslims of Assam opposed the formation of AAMSU. In an appeal, the Asomiya Muslim Public Relation Committee stated that the formation of AAMSU was unnecessary and it would bring about division between indigenous communities and Muslim community (Thakur 2014, 26–27).

The AAMSU came into existence as an antithesis to AASU under the patronage of the Congress. On 3 March 1980, in a discussion with Prime Minister Indira Gandhi who visited Guwahati to meet the leaders of Assam Movement, the leaders of AAMSU declared their readiness to accept 1971 as the cut-off year for determination of illegal foreigners in Assam (Hussain 1993, 121). And within less than a year of the beginning of the Assam Movement, AAMSU emerged as a counterforce of AASU and a counter-movement was launched by AAMSU against Assam Movement on 26 May 1980, by observing 'Demand Day' throughout the state. On the Demand Day, in Howley town of Barpeta district, AAMSU organized a big rally where four persons were killed in police firing (Ahmed 1999, 153). Many allege that in the Howley rally AAMSU supporters shouted the slogan 'Jai Bangla' by taking the Bangladeshi national flag in their hands (Borpujari 1999, 50).

The formation of AAMSU was the institutionalization of Muslim opposition to Assam Movement. While AASU was demanding 1951 as the cut-off year for identifying illegal foreign nationals in Assam against the 1971 cut-off year wanted by the central government, AAMSU demanded that 25 March 1971 should be the 'base date' for detection of foreigners in Assam on the basis of Indo-Bangladesh Treaty, 1972. The Indira Gandhi-led central government was prompt to make AAMSU part of the negotiation on Assam Movement as the organization had accepted the proposal of Mrs Gandhi regarding the cut-off date. By making AAMSU a party in the table of negotiations, the Congress-led central government tried to show its concerns towards the causes of Muslims in Assam. However, the decision of the central government to include AAMSU in the discussions vis-à-vis the Assam Movement made the AASU anguished. AASU labelled AAMSU as the agents of illegal Bangladeshis living in Assam. There were reports of frequent clashes between the supporters of AASU and AAMSU during the movement period. For instance, while AASU was demanding discussion on the situation of Assam in the winter session of Parliament, a clash occurred during the strike between AASU and AAMSU in Dalgaon, Sonitpur. The state government had to impose curfew in that area on 18 November (Thakur 2014, 35).

Once AAMSU received patronization of the central government, the supporters of Assam Movement were quick to label AAMSU as the organization of illegal Bangladeshis. On the other hand, AAMSU openly aligned with the Jamiat, a religious organization, to oppose Assam Movement although it criticized AASU of being controlled by RSS. The organization mobilized and united the immigrant Muslim community against AASU and Assam Movement. In the whole process, the community, particularly those living in Brahmaputra Valley, started to believe that they were not recognized as Assamese, rather as illegal Bangladeshis, by the leaders and supporters of the movement despite their attempt to integrate with Assamese language, culture and society.

THE STATE'S ROLE

The large-scale and continuous illegal migration from East Pakistan to Assam since Independence had always been overlooked by the central government primarily encouraged the Hindus living in East Pakistan to migrate to India. The government at the centre, led by Congress or non-Congress parties, simply ignored this issue. The government urged the movement leadership to treat the 'displaced persons' from East Pakistan/Bangladesh as a special case. Behind the charade of 'displaced persons', the government actually sought to safeguard the Hindus who immigrated from East Pakistan/Bangladesh. However, the leadership of Assam Movement declined to distinguish the illegal foreigners on the basis of religion. The AASU's standpoint on the whole issue is visible from its letter dated 13 November 1980 sent by its general secretary Bhrigu Kumar Phukan to the home minister of India. The letter clearly stated:

> Only yesterday the Prime Minister mentioned the Assam problem in the NIC meeting and said that any solution must not harm the minorities. Will you kindly explain to the people of Assam how detection of foreigners, on the basis of 1951 NRC only to avoid harassment to any genuine Indian, would harm the Indian minorities irrespective of religion? On the other hand, in the last Delhi meeting you suggested that the 'displaced persons' should be given special treatment, implying thereby that religion should be a factor in the detection process. We are all opposed to it. If the Central Government adopts such an attitude, the unity of the different sections of Indians residing in Assam and belonging to different religious groups will be jeopardized. We can never allow such a situation to develop. The detention process, therefore, must be on the basis of the constitutional provisions and the 1951 NRC. (Ahmed 1999, 201–202)

IMPOSITION OF ILLEGAL MIGRANTS (DETERMINATION BY TRIBUNAL) ACT

The IMDT Act was the state's response to the Assam Movement. The IMDT Act, 1983, was to provide for the establishment of tribunals for the determination, in a fair manner, of the question whether a person is an illegal migrant to enable the central government to expel illegal migrants from India and for matters connected there with or incidental thereto. The Act set up tribunals in each district, which are to be presided over by retired district/additional district judges. Congress (I) was in power both at the Centre and the state at the time of its formulation. The Parliament passed the Act to address the issue raised by Assam Movement, that is, the identification and deportation of illegal foreigners from Assam. The central government led by Indira Gandhi formulated the Act in an objective to marginalize and weaken the movement by making the issue of illegal foreigners in Assam very complex. The core contention was around the IMDT Act, 1983, which was perceived as an obstacle for the identification of foreigners as it imposed the onus of identification of the foreigner on the complainants.

Besides making the process of identification and deportation of illegal foreigners from Assam very complex, the Act also divided the society on communal lines. The IM(DT) was an immigration Act and had no relation to majority or minority community. However, since the imposition of the Act on Assam, the Congress party had been openly defending in the state that the Act as a provision to safeguard the interests of the minorities. Again, during the days of the Assam Movement after the Act was implemented, Congress argued that it was for safeguarding the interests of the minorities from the movement. Yet again, after the signing of Assam Accord, Congress started to publicize that the Act was to safeguard the interests of the minorities from the clauses of the Accord. The Act became a tool at the hands of Congress to show its solidarity towards the minorities. The stance taken by the Congress clearly demonstrated as to why the Government at the center had formulated the Act and later used the same for vote bank politics. The imposition of IMDT Act on Assam thereby bolstered the position of the Congress in the state electorally as the minorities, particularly the immigrant Muslims, began to consider the party as an ally against the political parties and organizations who supported the Assam Movement. Against the Congress politics of vote bank via the IMDT Act, most of the political parties and non-political organizations of the state continuously demanded the repeal of the Act. Ever since Act was in force, the politics of Assam was sharply divided into pro- and anti-IMDT groups. The anti-IMDT group began to label the entire immigrant Muslim community of Assam as illegal Bangladeshis their support to the IMDT Act. This, led to further alienation of the legal and genuine immigrant Muslims from the greater Assamese society (Nath 2015).

THE ASSAM ACCORD

The Assam Accord was signed between the Prime Minister of India and the movement leaders on 15 August 1985, India's Independence Day. Thereby, it marked the end of six years of political turmoil in the state. As per the Accord, illegal aliens who had entered the state between January 1966 and March 1971 were to be disenfranchised for 10 years and those who came after March 1971 to be deported. Moreover, the IMDT Act, which was an obstacle to the process of identification of illegal foreigners in Assam and was considered as a safeguard by immigrant communities living in Assam, was not with-drawn by the government as a result of the signing of the Accord, although the movement leaders strongly demanded for its repeal. Both parties agreed on 25 March 1971 as the cut-off date to ascertain who the foreigners were. It was decided that immigrants from Bangladesh who crossed over to Assam after 1966 would be debarred from fran-chise for 10 years. The Assam Accord, however, failed to address this complex issue. From the heap of accumulated frustrations, whether among the ethnic Assamese or among various tribal communities trying to assert their identities, militancy was born and virtually every part of the region came to be caught up in its grip. The policies of the state, since Independence, had been apathetic and indifferent towards the inherent ethnic problems of the state. A convention of the Minority Coordination Committee attended by CRPC, AAMSU, Jamiat, Minority Yuva Parishad and Minority Forum of Assam held on 28–29 September 1985 at Guwahati, just after the signing of the Assam Accord, strongly opposed the Accord and resolved that 'the Convention considers the Accord detrimental to the interests and safety of the minorities living in Assam. It has created a fear psychosis in the minds of the minorities ...' (Ahmed 1999, 229–234). The Hindu fundamentalist organizations indirectly tried to influence the movement. But Muslim opposition to the movement was direct through organization like Jamiat, which finally led the process to form the All Assam Minority Student Union to counter the movement. And with the emergence of AAMSU and Anuwara Taimur being made the chief minister of Assam, the situation which ensued has been explained by Mosudul Hoque as follows:

> The incidents and publicity during the Assam movement hurt the minorities of Assam who for centuries lived together with the majority and shared common culture. The orthodoxy among the Muslims of Assam, particularly of upper Assam, started from here. The first thing was that Muslims became introvert. More number of Muslims began to participate in Janaja. Use of mike for Ajan, attempt to show Muslim solidarity, emphasis on Muslim dress also started from then. The Maulavis from north India started to visit Assam frequently. With the increase of the visit of Hindutva leaders and journalists, Mulla-Moulanas visit to Assam also increased proportionately. Ordinary Muslims began to spend lots of time in reading Quran and religious discussions in Masjids. Communal elements began to root in Muslim mentality. (Hoque 2007)

The Assam Accord failed not only in realizing the primary objective of the Assam Movement but also proved violently cantankerous. This difficulty, as Baruah notes, lay in the ambiguity in the phrase 'identity and heritage of the Assamese people' since this idea was not easy to implement.[1] This difficulty was all the more aggravated when tribal people, especially the Bodos, refused to be counted anymore as Assamese. In addition, the perceived failure of the Assam Movement in resolving Assam's immigration crisis led to the radicalization of Assamese subnationalism, giving it a separatist turn. And the Bodo demand for a separate Bodoland and their pursuit of a violent path to achieve this goal brought forcefully to the fore the problem encountered in seeking Assamese hegemony in a multi-ethnic situation. The Bodo separatism is a testimony to the failure of Assamese leadership in realizing that 'Assamese-ness' is a contested conception.

---

[1] This is evident from the government report on the subject; see Government of Assam (1988, 12–13).

In failing to select sufficiently sensitive exclusionary historical and cultural symbols, and in being insufficiently sensitive to the human impact of their policy demands as applied to 'foreigners' and 'indigenous' people alike, the leaders of the Assam movement contributed to the process of ethnicization of Assamese politics. (Baruah 1999, 175)

What should also be added is that the contradiction between the Assamese subnationalist vision putting emphasis on 'Assamese Assam' and the reality of multi-ethnic Assam greatly facilitated the breakup of colonial Assam.

RISE OF INSURGENCY

The Assam Movement spawned a culture of violence which led to the emergence of insurgency outfits in the state. The United Liberation Front of Assam (ULFA) was born as a radical offshoot of the Assam Movement. It made its appearance on 7 April 1979, two months before the AASU observed its first 12 hours' strike on 8 June 1979, to protest against illegal migration into Assam. The ULFA had its roots in the same sociopolitical and economic issues. Under the leadership of Paresh Barua (chief of staff), along with Arabinda Rajkhowa (chairman), Anup Chetia (general secretary) and Pradeep Gogoi (vice-chairman under detention since 8 April 1998), the ULFA operated in close coordination with AASU and AAGSP in its initial stage. Many of the ULFA leaders are from Upper Assam districts of Sivasagar, Lakhimpur, Jorhat, Tinsukia and Dibrugarh. Many of them belong to the Mangaldoi stock. The ULFA was organized as a liberation army with modern weapons and trained cadres. The 1983 elections and the period of the Congress state government under Hiteswar Saikia that followed was the time when ULFA made the most significant inroads into Assam politics. Undoubtedly, the counter-insurgency operations by the paramilitary forces and a series of partisan political moves, widely credited to the late state chief minister Hiteswar Saikia, contributed towards the rise of violent activities in the state. The ULFA brought to the fore the question of underdevelopment and of Assam being treated as a colonial hinterland. Therefore, the ULFA could extend its support base beyond the ethnic Assamese parameter. This is evident from the fact that its cadres were drawn from almost all segments of the state's indigenous population. The ULFA seems to have introduced into Assam politics the ideology of armed revolution and the agenda of secession. For the ULFA, moderate representations of Assam's interest were of no use. It claimed that 'the mass movement of the past and especially the illegal elections of 1983 prove beyond doubt that there is no so-called moderate road available to the people of Assam' (Barua 1994). It viewed the non-implementation of Assam Accord as one more piece of evidence of the central government's apathy in protecting the interests of the people of the state. Therefore, it stood for armed action, conspicuous brutality and exemplary violence.

The main aim and objective of ULFA was to establish scientific socialism in an independent Assam. It regarded the Yandaboo Treaty of 1826 between Burma and the British rulers of India, which incorporated Assam into British India, as the episode that marked the end of Assam's independence and hence sought to restore that independence (Dasgupta 2001). Indeed, the ULFA had distanced itself from the immigration issue, and focused on issues of security and development of the people living in Assam (Asom Basi), rather the Assamese people, in striking contrast to the mainstream of subnationalist discourse. Thus, its ideological premises were more related to comprehensive parameters. Numerous statements of ULFA leaders indicate that their notion of Assam is more territorial than ethnolinguistically exclusive. Gradually, the ULFA established ties with the Nationalist Socialist Council of Nagaland (NSCN). With the active support and help of the NSCN, it raised a small guerrilla army and procured weapons for waging the war of revolution. Since then, the ULFA has established contacts with various militant groups inimical to India including the LTTE and the Afghan Mujahideens fighting in Kashmir. It also seems to have received active political and material support from nations hostile to India, while others provide sanctuary, base, camps and transit routes (Dasgupta 2001). Taking advantage of the regional party AGP that came to power in the state, the ULFA got an opportunity to act on a parallel course with the connivance of the state government. Although the Congress eventually came to power under the leadership of Hiteswar Saikia, the government lacked popular legitimacy.

After Mrs Gandhi's death, the political stalemate was taken over by the new Prime Minister Rajiv Gandhi. He eventually entered into an accord with the students leading the Assam Movement. The 1985 Assam Accord paved the way for the dissolution of the assembly and holding of fresh elections.

CONCLUSION

The day 15 August 1985 marked the end of the Assam Movement and the beginning of a new era in the political history of Assam with far-reaching consequences. The six years' movement was a watershed for politics in Assam and the following elections led to a reconfiguration of the party system in the state. The principal actors behind the Assam Movement recast themselves into a new political party called Asom Gana Parishad. Rajiv Gandhi's strategy of entering into an accord with the moderate elements did not bring extremism to an end. Rather it resulted in the loss of Congress at the polls. The political scenario in the state had substantially changed with the emergence of an alternative regional party, that is, the AGP, which challenged the hegemonic status of the Congress party.

We turn in the next chapter to discussing the rise of regional party formation in the state after the long Congress rule.

REFERENCES

Ahmed, S. U. 1999. *Muslims in Assam (1200–2000)*. Nagaon: Marigold Compu Print.

Baruah, Sanjib. 1986. 'Immigration, Ethnic Conflict and Political Turmoil: Assam 1979–1985'. *Asian Survey* 26 (11): 1184–1206.

———. 1999. *India against Itself: Assam and the Politics of Nationality*. New Delhi: Oxford University Press, 128–129.

Basu, A., and A. Kohli, eds. 1998. *Community Conflicts and the State in India*. New Delhi: Oxford University Press.

Borpujari, H. K. 1999. *Uttor-Purbanchalor Xomosya aaru Rajniti* (in Assamese) [Probelms and Politics of North-East]. Guwahati: G L Publication.

Dasgupta, A. 2001. 'Small Arms Proliferation in India's North-East: A Case Study of Assam'. *Economic & Political Weekly* 36 (1, 6 January): 59–65.

Dutta, Nandana. 2012. *Questions of Identity in Assam: Location, Migration, Hybridity.* New Delhi: SAGE Publications.

Gohain, Hiren. 1980. *On the Present Movement in Assam.* Calcutta: Sribhumi Publishing.

Government of Assam. 1988. 'Implementation of Assam Accord'. Available at: https://assamaccord.assam.gov.in/portlets/the-assam-accord

Gupta, Sekhar. 1984. *Assam: A Valley Divided.* New Delhi: Vikas Publishing House.

Hoque, Mosudul. 2007. 'Asom Andolan aru Sankhyaloghur Somosya'. In *Asom Andolan: Pratishruti and Phalashruti* (in Assamese; Assam Movement: Promises and Results), edited by Hiren Gohain and Dilip Bora, 299–318. Guwahati: Banalata.

Hussain, Monirul. 1993. *The Assam Movement: Class, Ideology and Identity.* New Delhi: Manak Publishers.

Kimura, Makiko. 2003. 'Memories of the Massacre: Violence and Collective Identity in the Narratives on the Nellie Incident'. *Asian Ethnicity* 4 (2): 225–239.

Nath, Manoj Kumar. 2015. *Axom Andolan: Potobhumi, Itihas, Bortoman* (in Assamese; Assam Movement: Background, History, Present). Guwahati: Aank Baak Publishers.

———. 2015. *Asomor Rajnitit Musalman: Biswas, Bastob aru Sanghat* (in Assamese; Muslims in Politics of Assam: Myth, Reality and Conflict). Guwahati: Banalata.

———. 2016. 'Communal Politics in Assam: Growth of AIUDF since 2006'. *Economic & Political Weekly* 51 (16): 88–93.

Prabhakara, M. S. 2005, July. 'Understanding a Controversial Legislation'. *The Hindu.*

Thakur, G. C. 2014. *Asom Andolanor Dinponji* (in Assamese; Diary of Assam Movement). Guwahati: Astha Publications.

Asom Gana Parishad and Competitive Politics

The political scenario in the post-Congress polity was dominated by two streams of political forces: at the national level BJP emerged as an alternative, while in many states, the vacuum created by the decline of Congress was filled by the state-based regional parties drawing upon a relatively narrow social base. With the Congress dominance under challenge, state politics began to receive greater attention and Indian politics increasingly became more state-specific. This fundamental change gave rise to a number of related changes with enormous implications for the states. It introduced multiparty competitions, thereby changing the structure of electoral competition in the states. This provided space for the rise of new social identities based on ethnicity and community, which gave regional parties a greater role in national politics and loosened the tight mould of federalism, creating thereby a tendency towards decentralization. (Palshikar 2015). The long-standing influence Congress held in Assam was challenged by a regional party, namely the AGP, in the mid-1980s. The AGP was born in October 1985 as a result of a long-drawn or sustained social movement. The movement had articulated the regional aspirations of the Assamese people, which culminated in the formation of this party. The principal actors behind the Assam Movement recast themselves into this new political party two months after the signing of the historic Assam Accord. Another two months later, AGP won a decisive victory in the elections to the state assembly and formed the first government by a regional party in Assam. The AGP emerged as an alternative to the Congress party in the state. However, the seeds of a viable regional political party for the first time were sown way back in the late 70s. Although the Assam Movement that preceded the formation of a regional political party was launched apparently on the issue of illegal immigration and the threat to Assamese identity, the grievances articulated by the movement included larger issues of neglect suffered by the state which ultimately converted the state into a colonial hinterland.

The emergence of AGP was a significant development in the politics of Assam after a long Congress rule in the state (Goswami 2013). The hegemony of the Congress was broken, and several new parties have emerged since then. The party found it difficult to compete with its rival that projected itself as a party unfolding the interest of the people of the state. For all national parties, the 1985 election marked a significant decline in strength (Table 4.1).

Thus, the rise and consolidation of power by the AGP had a profound impact on the politics of the state. The AGP made an impressive victory in the 1985 election and Prafulla Kumar Mahanta became the

Table 4.1 *Performance of Political Parties in 1985 Assam Assembly Elections*

Name of the Parties	No. of Seats Contested	No. of Seats Won	Percentage Secured
INC	125	25	24.47
AGP	105	63	34.54
BJP	85	–	1.45
JP	73	4	3.20
ICS	34	–	1.07
CPM	38	2	4.34
UMF	56	17	10.85
PTCA	27	3	3.64
CPI	20	–	0.99
LKD	19	–	0.23
UTNLF	15	1	–
IND	533	10	16.22
Total	1,128	125	100.00

Source: Government of Assam, State Election Office.

chief minister, the youngest ever in Indian history. After becoming chief minister, he lost no time to declare that the AGP's victory meant a victory of 'regionalism with a nationalist outlook' (*India Today* 1986).

The politics in the state has begun to reflect the political logic of the state's multi-ethnic reality and social deepening of democratization. Unlike most other Indian states where regionalism is being articulated in terms of one dominant cultural community, in Assam a number of smaller ethnic communities have begun to carve out areas of influence through their respective parties (Barua and Goswami 1999).

RISE OF ASSAMESE NATIONALISM AND SHIFT IN POLITICS

The emergence of AGP heralded a new era in Assam politics. The electoral politics in Assam has seen a new trend since 1985 and this has served to shape the political history of Assam. The first regional formation, that is, the AGP came to power riding on a wave of Assamese subnationalism. A new brand of educated, young men and women, including large numbers of graduates, teachers, lawyers, entered the political arena and emerged as the leaders or representatives of people's interests. The leadership of AGP has remained mainly in the hands of middle class from the urban area. The party owes its political existence to regional issues. The 1985 election was critical for Assam, as it led to a reconfiguration of the party system and a durable realignment of social groups with political parties (Goswami 2003a). This election led to a very high level of popular participation and enthusiasm. Subregional parties such as Autonomous State Demand Committee (ASDC) and United Minority Front (UMF) articulating the interests of smaller ethnic and cultural communities have also made their presence felt. Thus, linguistic nationalism mixed with tribal nationalism has added a new dimension to Assam politics. The new political outfit (AGP) succeeded in mobilizing its core Assamese-dominated constituency in a big way and won a clear majority. The turnout of voters in the election jumped to 79 per cent, 12 percentage points up from the previous record set in the 1978 elections. Although the AGP rode on a wave to power on the foreigners' issue, it needs to be mentioned that even in its moment of glory, the AGP could secure less than 35 per cent of total votes and manage to win only 65 seats, just one more than the bare minimum required for a majority in the assembly (Yadav 2001). The party did emerge as the focal point of non-Congress mobilization and pushed the national parties to the sidelines. At the same time, this success underlined the limitations of its catchment area. The Congress won 25 seats and polled 23 per cent votes. Part of the reason behind AGP's victory was that during the election the pro-Assamese national-ist votes remained solidly behind the AGP, but the votes of the forces inimical to the movement got divided, with the UMF capturing 17 seats and securing 12 per cent of votes.

In this election, CPI could not win any seat and only two could be bagged by the CPM. However, the Left parties had put up a remarkable performance during the post-Emergency assembly elections of 1978 with the CPM winning 11 seats and the CPI 5. The Revolutionary Communist Party of India (RCPI) too won four seats in the elec-tions. The PTCA won three seats in Bodo areas and the United Tribal National Liberation Front (UTNLF) another tribal party, won a single seat. Ethnic nationalism was a powerful political force in this era.

Although no direct survey data is available for this crucial assembly election, broad inferences can be drawn by analysing results taking into consideration the social background of various constituencies. The assembly constituencies have been divided into four broad cat-egories: those with dominance of Bengali immigrants, those where the STs are dominant, those of Upper Assam dominated by the tea-tribes and those dominated by the dominant ethnic Assamese community. A look at the constituency-wise analysis of this election shows that the turnout was exceptionally high in the immigrant areas and lowest in the tea-tribe-dominated areas. AGP performed best in the areas dominated by the ethnic Assamese community and the tea-tribes. It managed to get a respectable share of votes and a few seats in the immigrant and the tribal areas as well, presumably by mobilizing the Assamese minority population. Most of the UMF votes were concentrated in the immigrant constituencies and the PTCA secured votes almost exclusively in the tribal areas. Squeezed from both the ends, the Congress did poorly every-where, especially among the immigrant areas, and could save its face only in the tea-growing areas with 34 per cent votes and 9 seats (Table 4.2).

Table 4.2 Category-wise Analysis of Assembly Elections in Assam, 1985

Region/District	Seats	Turnout (%)	AGP Won/Contested	Vote %	Congress Won/Contested	Vote %	UMFA Won/Contested	Vote %	ICS Won/Contested	Vote %
1	2	3	4	5	6	7	8	9	10	11
Immigrants	15	87.6	4/14	21.7	1/15	12.8	6/13	33.1	1/10	6.3
Tea-growing areas	29	73.8	19/29	41.0	9/29	33.9	0/6	1.5	0/18	0.8
ST dominated	19	77.8	9/12	25.9	2/19	21.4	1.5	3.1	1/11	3.8
Others	63	80.0	33/56	38.4	13/62	22.2	11/36	13.3	2/33	3.2
Total	126	79.2	65/111	35.0	25/125	23.2	18/60	12.1	4/72	3.2

(Continued)

Table 4.2 *Continued*

Region/District	Left Parties		PCTA		Other Parties		Independent	
	Won/Contested	Vote %	Won/Contested	Vote %	Won/Contested	Vote %	Won/Contested	Vote %
	12	13	14	15	16	17	18	19
Immigrants	1/8	8.0	0/0	0.0	0/18	2.3	2/38	15.8
Tea-growing areas	0/12	4.0	0/7	2.6	0/40	3.1	1.171	13.1
ST-dominated	0/8	4.0	3/12	17.2	0/13	1.9	3/69	22.7
Others	1/32	6.2	0/9	1.2	0/73	3.2	3/255	12.3
Total	2/60	5.7	3/28	3.6	0/144	2.8	9/533	14.4

Source: CSDS Data Unit.

Note: The classification of Assembly constituencies used in this and subsequent tables has been developed by the author on the basis of local political information and available estimates. The ST-dominated constituencies were identified on the basis of the proportion of ST population in the constituency and not just on whether the constituency was reserved for ST or not. The category 'other' parties includes mainly areas dominated by Asomiya Hindus.

END OF ONE PARTY DOMINANCE ERA

The 1985 election in Assam signalled the end to the one-party dominance by the Congress system and gave way to a bipolar competition
between the Congress and the AGP. A close look at the verdict reveals
that it was far from instituting a two-party system. Put together, the
two big parties did not command even 60 per cent of the popular vote.
The Congress rainbow coalition had begun to come apart and each
slice was headed in a different direction. What the 1985 election had
instituted was a system of high mobilization and intense competition
among diverse social groups—a competition that has introduced and
sustained party fragmentation (Yadav 2001). The subsequent elections demonstrated this fact. It is seen that small states have been a
clear advantage for the party at the Centre, for smaller the state, the
greater is its dependence on the Centre. It is exactly because of this
that a regional party, if it wishes to replace the party at the Centre,
must exert itself to prove its credentials through hard work, honesty
and a clear-sighted approach to the concerned state's economic and
political problems. Unfortunately, the AGP has displayed none of these
qualities in its four years in office. Instead of making a sincere attempt
to cleanse public life of the prevailing corruption and misgovernance
that had ensnarled it during the previous Congress (I) regime, the AGP
leadership itself got entangled in the coils of corruption and one scandal after another hit the party. Instead of trying to do away with the
debased Congress (I) culture, the AGP leaders, except a few, adopted
a lifestyle which sharply distanced them from the people. This lifestyle
has been resented by people who have been harassed by devastating
recurrent floods, collapsing administrative set-up, disrupted communication lines, totally incompetent village development schemes,
a demoralized police force and, to top it all, ever-growing ethnic and
other forms of violence (Goswami 2013)

As a regional party during its four years in office, the AGP failed to
draw up any comprehensive plan for the socio-economic development
of the state. On the contrary, it has allowed its bureaucracy to interfere
upon by both AGP and AASU leaders at all possible levels and has
taken no steps to prevent the drift in the state's law and order situation.
During its initial years in power, the AGP thought it wise not to have

any meaningful liaison with the national Opposition parties. It even followed a policy of confrontation with Opposition-sponsored programmes as was evidenced by its attitude towards the all-India strike called by the combined Opposition soon after the AGP assumed office. It was only when the state problems started mounting that the AGP discovered the need of seeking the cooperation of the Opposition parties. Its earlier policy of keeping up the struggle against the Congress (I) at the state level while at the same time keeping New Delhi pleased did not pay much dividend and the votaries of a pro-Congress (I) line within the AGP got outnumbered. The escalation of violence and the vexed minority problem in the state coupled with the Centre's attempt to financially strangulate the state left the AGP with no choice but to draw closer to the national Opposition parties. AGP became a valued component of the National Front that came to power, though briefly in 1989. Clearly, AGP's drawing closer to the non-Congress (I) parties was necessitated by the political compulsions of the state. Another factor which pushed the AGP towards the National Front was its growing differences with the AASU.

The AASU has been in the need to chart an independent course in the state's politics and has taken conscious steps to distance itself from the ruling party and shed its image of being a youth wing of the AGP. It realized the error of openly aligning itself with AGP during the 1985 polls. Likewise, the AGP realized the dangers of relying too much on AASU. Such dependence on the student organization had already eaten into the credibility of AGP as a political party. It, therefore, thought it wise to shed its isolationist, regional image and come close to the national parties. Having become a constituent of the National Front, the AGP had little to lose and much to gain in the then immediate future. However, in its four years in office it also failed to build up any grassroots organization worth the name in the peasant or youth front. With AGP's perceived inefficacy on the foreigners' issue and allegation of corruption, and its lack of concern to the issues that agitated the minds of different social segments, the appeal of the regional party eroded rather rapidly (Misra 1990b).

Moreover, the sense of deprivation was deeper among the Bodo tribal communities in the late 1980s, nourished by the failure of the AGP government to do anything for the Bodos despite the fact that the All Bodo Students' Union (ABSU) had thrown its full support to the Assam Movement. Soon after it came to power, the new government declared all encroachments made after 1 January 1980 as illegal in accordance with Assam Accord (Clause 10: Prevention of Encroachment of Government Lands). In effect, it became eviction of tribals from the land on which they were settled without formal pattas. The ostensible reason was a desire to protect the forest lands, but the policy was implemented without regard to the political consequences of such an action or ensuring that there were adequate alternative provisions made for the people living on these lands. Such an attempt to evict illegal settlers from the protected forests also included the eviction of some Bodos, providing a significant spark to the Bodo Movement (Hazarika 1994). The breakdown of trust has to a great extent been the fault of AGP government. It displayed a great degree of insensitivity towards tribals' feelings in the choice of policies, which it had placed high on its list of priorities in the first year of office (Goswami 2001). As the assertion of the Assamese subnationalism became vocal and politically overbearing, the Bodo people were reminded of their own distinctive sociocultural identity. They too began to assert themselves politically by demanding a distinct homeland for themselves through subregional parties. At times they compromised their ethnic character by merging with national mainstream parties such as the BJP or the Congress party, which are known for their integrationist positions.

The ABSU had gained recognition as a more radical representative of the interests of the Bodo community. It gained more prominence with its demand for a separate state from Assam for the ethnic Bodos, by dividing Assam on the basis of what they called '50:50'. Along with the democratic protest actions, violent activities also started. 'Divide Assam 50:50' became a familiar slogan alarming the ethnic Assamese, heartening to those tribals who wanted a separate identity. The youthful elements became prominent both in the planning and organization of such a campaign. One could see here an uncanny similarity with the Assam Movement, and ironically, it was directed against the Assamese leaders of AGP who were in power at that time. This time the onus was on the regionalist AGP to unleash state terror to suppress a subregional popular movement that was seeking to gain regional autonomy

(Dasgupta 1998). It was widely behaved that the Congress party had a hand in stoking the fire in order to trouble the first AGP government. The Bodo Movement for a separate state severely destabilized the AGP government, impelled by which the state government dealt with the movement with vengeance.

AGP AND THE 1991 ELECTIONS

The next trial of electoral strength took place not in 1989, as in the rest of country, but in 1991 as disturbances prevailed in Assam. AGP suffered a humiliating defeat in the assembly elections of 1991. Its vote share of 17.9 per cent was practically half of what it got during the 1985 wave. The Congress staged a comeback by winning 65 seats and securing clear majority. The comeback was remarkable, not for the size of its majority, but for the recovery staged in the aftermath of the Assam Movement. In terms of popular vote share, the verdict could not actually reflect a resurgence of support for the Congress. The main reasons for the Congress victory, despite poor vote share, were the division of the pro-Assamese nationalist votes between the AGP and Natun Asom Gana Parishad (NAGP; *natun* meaning 'new' in Assamese), a breakaway faction of the AGP, and the unprecedented performance of the BJP. NAGP won five seats with 5.5 per cent votes. Since the NAGP and the BJP appealed to the same social constituency as the AGP, their performance was bound to affect the electoral prospects of the AGP very badly. The BJP which was never before a significant force won 10 seats and polled 6.4 per cent votes. While the AGP and the NAGP together polled 23.6 per cent, the BJP's 6.4 per cent votes in 47 constituencies spread all over the state must have cut into the vote share of the non-Congress forces. It could be argued that the three formations put together had polled more votes than the Congress, but this fact was no more than a statistical consolidation (Yadav 2001). Therefore, the seats won by the Congress in 1991 Lok Sabha elections need not necessarily mean an improvement in its support base. The Congress managed to win eight seats with 28.5 per cent votes compared to only four seats with 28.5 per cent votes that it won in the 1985 elections (Table 4.3). Like its performance in the assembly elections, in the Lok Sabha elections

Table 4.3 *Performance of Political Parties in 1991 Lok Sabha Elections*

Name of the Parties	No. of Seats Contested	No. of Seats Won	Percentage Secured
INC	14	8	28.49
AGP	14	1	17.62
BJP	8	2	9.60
CPI	4	–	2.15
CPM	2	1	4.73
JD	6	–	5.16
JP	6	–	0.72
JD(S)	2	–	0.03
IPF	1	–	0.31
RCPI(BR)	1	–	0.11
NAGP	11	–	5.85
ASDC	1	1	1.65
ICS	5	–	2.15
AJD	2	–	0.10
AJP	1	–	0.09
URMCA	9	–	2.02
GGS	1	–	0.09
PTCA	2	–	1.03
UMF	4	–	2.49
SLP	2	–	1.49
DDP	2	1	0.12
IND	69		14.00
Total	167	14	100.00

Source: Government of Assam, State Election Office, Dispur, 28 April 1992.

too, BJP performed well bagging two seats with 9.6 per cent votes. That the political balance in the state shifted a great deal is evident from the fact that the BJP emerged as the third largest party in the state after Congress and AGP. The election results clearly reflect the fragmentation of Assam politics.

This election also proved that the decline of the Left forces was not a temporary phenomenon. The Communist Party of India (Marxist)—CPI(M)—won two and the CPI four seats in these elections. Among the parties representing ethnic minorities, the newly formed ASDC of Karbi Anglong district won four assembly seats with 1.6 per cent votes. Other such parties drew a blank (Table 4.4). The assembly elections could also not be held in time for the same reason. The end of AGP rule in 1990 and beginning of Congress rule in 1991, however, did not expedite the realization of an independent Bodoland state. Ultimately the leadership gave up the demand for a separate state and agreed to have autonomy under the provision of the Bodo Accord 1993.

The scenario at the parliamentary level was not much different from that of the assembly elections. At the parliamentary level, the AGP won

Table 4.4 *Performance of Political Parties in 1991 Assam Assembly Election*

Name of the Parties	No. of Seats Contested	No. of Seats Won	Percentage Secured
INC	124	65	28.98
AGP	120	19	18.07
BJP	47	10	6.42
NAGP	85	5	5.50
JD	95	1	4.81
CPI	37	4	2.46
CPM	28	2	3.87
ASDC	8	4	1.61
ICS	45	–	1.46
URMCA	54	–	1.32
UMF	29	–	1.31
PTCA	15	–	1.07
Others	108	–	1.52
IND	855	15	21.60
Total	1,650	125	100.00

Source: Government of Assam, State Election Office.

only a single seat with 17.6 per cent votes. The NAGP could not win any seat but polled a significant 5.9 per cent votes. There was significant erosion of AGP votes in all categories of seats except in the ST seats where it somewhat retained its votes. NAGP played a spoiler for AGP, especially in the Assamese-dominated areas including tea gardens areas.

FACTIONALISM AND UPSURGE OF INSURGENT ACTIVITIES

The disaster that overtook the AGP in this election was predictable. The unseemly wrangles among top leaders of the AGP and the rampant factionalism had culminated in the split in the party and thereby led to the defeat of AGP in the election. The other factor that contributed in eroding the regional image of the AGP was the sudden upsurge in the activities of the ULFA.

Indeed, the emergence of ULFA turned out to be the nemesis of AGP government, which was causally related to some of the failures that arose out of the debris of the AGP leaders. Taking advantage of the AGP being in power, the ULFA got an opportunity to act on a parallel course for gaining independence for Assam with the connivance of the state government. In the process, the ULFA entered into a rather complex sort of relationship with the state authority. The AGP leaders' ambivalence regarding ULFA, which they could neither suppress nor make a deal with, left them with no escape route when finally crackdown from above came. The deteriorating law and order situation in the state enabled the Centre finally to impose President's rule prematurely in November 1990 and declared ULFA an unlawful organization under Unlawful Activities (Prevention) Act 1967 (Roy, Miri, and Goswami 1997).

CATEGORY-WISE ANALYSIS

The category-wise analysis (Table 4.5) shows that there was a substantial erosion of AGP votes in all categories of seats, except in the ST areas where the party somehow retained its votes. The NAGP played the spoiler for the AGP, especially in the Assamese-dominated areas,

Table 4.5 Category-wise Analysis of Assembly Elections in Assam, 1991

Region/District	Seats	Turnout (%)	AGP Won/ Contested	AGP Vote %	Congress Won/ Contested	Congress Vote %	NAGP Won/ Contested	NAGP Vote %	BJP Won/ Contested	BJP Vote %
1	2	3	4	5	6	7	8	9	10	11
Immigrants	15	83.1	1/14	9.2	9/15	30.4	0/7	1.9	1/5	6.7
Tea-growing Areas	29	70.3	0/29	18.8	27/29	44.4	0/25	6.8	0/11	1.0
ST-dominated	19	73.0	4/16	16.9	4/18	22.0	1.8	3.4	1/2	0.2
Others	63	75.1	15/61	20.1	26/62	25.2	4/45	6.4	9/31	10.8
Total	126	74.7	19/120	17.9	66/124	29.2	5/85	5.5	10/49	6.7

Region/District	Left Parties		ASDC		Other Parties		Independent	
	Won/Contested	Vote %	Won/Contested	Vote %	Won/Contested	Vote %	Won/Contested	Vote %
	12	13	14	15	16	17	18	19
Immigrants	2/5	8.4	0/0	0.0	0/48	17.1	3/77	26.3
Tea-growing areas	2/15	6.1	0/1	0.2	0/73	8.7	0/	13.1
ST-dominated	0/8	4.0	3/12	17.2	0/13	1.9	3/69	22.7
Others	1/32	6.2	0/9	1.2	0/73	3.2	3/255	12.3

Source: CSDS Data Unit.

including the tea belt. The BJP took a significant slice of the anti-migrant voters in the immigrant-dominated areas, thus making things difficult for the AGP. For the first time, the BJP registered its presence in the state in the Assamese- as well as immigrant-dominant areas.

An analysis of the constituency-wise performance of the Congress party shows that, in this election, Congress's performance was much better in the areas dominated by non-Assamese population. Out of the 65 seats it won, at least 40 were constituencies where *Ana Asomiya* (non-Assamese) tea garden labour population was electorally significant. Its biggest gains were concentrated in the tea-growing areas. It also gained heavily in the immigrant areas, thus indicating that it won back the support of immigrant Muslims. The Congress benefited in the Assamese-dominated areas where it doubled its seats, mainly due to the split of votes caused by the NAGP's presence. The Congress made a clean sweep in the traditional stronghold, tea-growing areas. The Congress returned to power in 1991, though not in its traditional role as a party representing a rainbow social coalition of all the major communities of Assam.

AGP'S INCLUSIVE STRATEGY AND THE 1996 ELECTIONS

In 1996, Lok Sabha elections were held simultaneously with the state elections. The AGP had realized the inherent limitations of its social constituency and therefore set in motion the process of realignment of political forces in the state (Goswami 2001b). The most important political development was that AGP came to understand the importance of keeping at least some minority groups with it. Meanwhile, the AGP and NAGP and the other Opposition parties, including the Left parties, as also the ASDC and the BODO People's Party (Sangsuma) BPP(S), and even the UMF which claimed to represent the interests of the religious and linguistic minorities, joined hands with AGP. Thus major sections of the Left, regional forces and ethnic and religious minorities stood solidly behind the AGP-led alliance. AGP managed to garner the militants' support with a promise to vouch for the cause of self-determination which incidentally amounted to accepting the demand for secession of Assam, in accordance with ULFA's political parlance. AGP, therefore, in its election manifesto of 1996 had placed more emphasis on the question of 'greater autonomy' and the 'right to self-determination' for the state. Surprisingly, the foreign national issue and implementation of the Assam Accord were not included in the AGP manifesto, particularly because of the alliances it had to form to keep the non-Congress votes together. It was interesting to note that except the BJP, none of the parties including AGP really harped on the issue of the detection and deportation of 'foreigners' though most of them insisted that immigration from Bangladesh should be stopped. The BJP was the only party which advocated the pre-1985 AGP line. But this issue never really took off because its main vehicle, AGP, decided to play it down. The experience of five years in power and five years in opposition seemed to have helped AGP to learn some lessons. It realized that it could not rule Assam without securing the support of non-Assamese population. Its silence on the issue of detection and deportation of immigrants, during the campaign period, as reflected in its manifesto, indicated this realization.

The new inclusive strategy of the AGP had three components: (a) AGP under Mahanta's leadership accepted back the dissenting faction led by Bhrigu Kumar Phukon; (b) the party entered into a political coalition with the Left and (c) the party underscored the need for a social coalition. This new inclusive strategy paid rich dividends in the final outcome of both the assembly and Lok Sabha elections. The AGP succeeded in regaining a majority in the state assembly. On its own, the party's tally of 61 fell a little short of the majority mark of 64, but its Left allies (including the ASDC, a Marxist–Leninist group) contributed another 10 seats and thus gave it a clear majority. The party improved its vote share dramatically compared to the debacle of 1991. The return of the NAGP helped the party not only to recover the 6 per cent votes that it had taken away, but also in improving its vote share by another few points. Eventually the party secured 30 per cent votes, about 12 percentage points higher than its vote share in previous election. This performance appears less impressive than its historic victory in 1985, but it needs to be remembered that the AGP contested only 99 seats this time. Its partners, the CPI, the CPI(M) and

Table 4.6 *Performance of Political Parties in 1996 Assam Assembly Elections*

Name of the Parties	No. of Seats Contested	No. of Seats Won	Percentage Secured
INC	122	34	30.56
AGP	96	59	29.70
BJP	117	4	10.41
CPI	11	3	1.96
CPM	10	2	1.94
AIIC(T)	106	2	3.70
JD	32	–	0.56
JP	2	–	0.01
Samata Party	1	–	0.00
ASDC	5	5	1.98
ICS	8	–	0.12
Samajwadi	12	–	0.04
Shiv Sena	5	–	0.03
CPI(ML)	5	–	0.16
AB	5	–	0.01
URMCA	9	–	0.17
UMF	19	2	1.12
RCPI(RB)	6	–	0.06
IND	657	11	17.47
Total	1,228	122	100.00

Source: Government of Assam, State Election Office, Dispur, 12 December 1996.

the ASDC secured another 6 percentage points. The Congress tally was reduced to half, despite the fact that the party improved its vote share slightly. This was a clear effect of the 'Opposition unity' that it had to confront. The same pattern was repeated in the Lok Sabha elections held about the same time. The Congress and the AGP won five seats each. One seat went to an independent candidate. Compared to 1991, the Congress lost three seats and the BJP lost one. AGP gained four seats. CPI(M), ASDC and independents retained their one seat each. Compared to the 1991 elections, the Congress lost four seats to the AGP but it won one seat from the BJP. Thus Congress's loss proved to be AGP's gain. The alliance ensured a strong presence for AGP in all the regions of the state since it had forged a rainbow coalition cutting across ethnic lines.

CATEGORY-WISE ANALYSIS

The category-wise analysis (Table 4.7) explains the anatomy of this election. The AGP gained back some Muslim support in the immigrant areas and made its principal gains in the ethnic Assamese-dominated and tea-growing areas. It did not secure any significant gains in the ST constituencies. Its gains were evenly spread out except for the tribal-dominated area. The Congress's major loss of votes and seats was in the tea-growing areas. However, the party led in these areas over the AGP alliance in terms of votes, though it trailed the alliance in all other areas. The election also saw the splitting of the tribal votes with a strong showing by independents in these seats. The Congress seemed to retain its influence among the immigrants though it won only 4 out of the 15 seats in these areas.

The unity of the major non-Congress parties of regional and leftist orientations played a decisive role, particularly in the tribal dominated areas of the state. These areas had been traditional Congress bastions in which the party could dominate till 1985. But in this election the non-Congress alliance could defeat the party in constituencies such as Baithalangsu, Halflong, Dhipu, Gossaigaon, Sidli and Udalguri (Goswami 2001b). In the Karbi areas, ASDC won all the five seats. In the Bodo areas, independents owing allegiance to the various Bodo factions, which were part of the non-Congress Opposition, won seven seats and AGP won the other two seats. In the Karbi areas ASDC's margin over the Congress was so high that the latter appeared to be losing its electoral significance. In the Bodo areas the winning margins were not very high because of the fact that in those areas no dominant tribal party had emerged. The tribal votes thus were divided. Nevertheless they went against the Congress. The result of this election

Table 4.7 Category-wise Analysis of Assembly Elections in Assam, 1996

			AGP		Congress		BJP		Left	
Region/District	Seats	Turnout (%)	Won/ Contested	Vote %	Won/ Contested	Vote %	Won/ Contested	Vote %	Won/ Contested	Vote %
1	2	3	4	5	6	7	8	9	10	11
Immigrants	15	84.7	4/10	21,3	4/15	29.6	0/13	10.4	2/6	10.4
Tea-growing areas	29	74.6	11/24	30.2	16/29	40-0	0/29	6.8	1/6	8.6
ST-dominated	19	80.4	5/12	18.4	1/19	22.1	0/16	3.4	0/0	5.3
Others	63	77.9	41/53	35.5	15/63	29.9	4/63	6.4	2/10	3.7
Total	126	78.3	61/99	30.1	66/124	30.7	4/121	10.3	5/22	4.0

Region/District	ASDC		INC(T)		Other Parties		Independent	
	Won/ Contested	Vote %	Won/ Contested	Vote %	Won/ Contested	Vote %	Won/ Contested	Vote %
	12	13	14	15	16	17	18	19
Immigrants	0/0	8.4	0/0	0.0	0/48	17.1	3/77	26.3
Tea-growing areas	0/0	6.1	0/1	0.2	0/73	8.7	0/	13.1
ST-dominated	5/5	4.0	3/12	17.2	0/13	1.9	3/69	22.7
Others	0/0	6.2	0/9	1.2	0/73	3.2	3/255	12.3
Total	5/5	1.9	2/111	3.7	2/108	2.2	11/658	17.1

Source: CSDS Data Unit.

exposed the myth that in Assam the Congress influence over tribals was overwhelming.

In the immigrant areas also, the alliance proved to be effective. In these areas, out of a total of 15 seats, the Congress won 4, AGP 4, CPI(M) 2, UMF 2, CPI 1, Congress(T) 1 and PDF 1. Thus the AGP and the Congress did equally well. Even their vote shares remained more or less equal. It is interesting to note that the UMF, claiming to represent minority interest and particularly that of the immigrant minority, could win only two seats in the region. The experience of the five years of AGP rule, when there were no riots and when no real attempts were made to deport the immigrant settlers of the 'chars', must have motivated the immigrant population to try its luck with the front. UMF's failure to make an impact could be understood in terms of the general feeling among Assam voters that political parties do not care specially for particular communities.

It has often been held that the tea belt has been the preserve of the Congress, and during the last decade, the Congress party has been able to retain its hold over the main component of this region, that is, the tea labourer community. Even during the AGP's wave in 1985, these voters helped the Congress win the Dibrugarh parliamentary seat comfortably. In fact, the Assam Chah Mazdoor Sangha, an affiliate of INTUC, has been organizing the tea labourers of Assam since 1947. The organizational strength of INTUC in the tea belt of Brahmaputra Valley had been the prime reason for the Congress dominance in this region (Goswami and Sharma 1993). However, the situation seems to have changed radically. The BJP, CPI and AGP have been trying to get a foothold in this region. The AGP, in fact, started the Assam Chah Sramik Parishad to counter the INTUC. For example, in Chabua area 15,000 tea workers were reported to have left the INTUC-controlled Assam Chah Mazdur Sangha to join Assam Chah Sramik Parishad. AASU too had been trying to influence the Tea Tribes Student Organization for quite some time. In the 1996 assembly elections, of the total 29 of such tea community-dominant constituencies, the Congress won 16 seats with the AGP bagging away 11 and the CPI 1. The AGP thus made inroads into the Congress bastion.

Table 4.8 *Party Preference among Various Castes/Communities/Groups (Row Percentage), 1996*

Caste/Community	AGP + Alliance	Congress	BJP
Upper Caste	45/0	5.0	50.0
OBC	46.9	23.5	28.4
SC	66.7	22.2	11.1
ST	33.3	38.1	19.0
Muslims	25.0	50.0	–
Others	–	75.0	25.0

Source: CSDS Data Unit.

The post-poll survey data clearly present details of AGP's newly found voter base pitted against that of the Congress and the BJP (Table 4.8). It confirms that the AGP's inclusive strategy had succeeded in splitting Muslim votes and securing a good chunk of the SC and OBC vote bank for the AGP and its allies.

CONCLUSION

The advantage secured by the AGP as a result of historical and political exigencies to unite the people for forming a cohesive Assamese nationality could not be capitalized by the party. It is now universally acknowledged that the party has failed to fulfil its historic role. Conventional dissent could be managed by suitable re-apportionment of political office, though there is necessarily a limit to such compromises. Since the Assam Movement had, from its very origin, a militant component and confused ideas for an independent Assam (*Swadhin Assam*) with 'class struggle', ready to make common cause to achieve this synthesis with the very social forces that were the principal 'object' of Assam Movement, these contradictions could never be resolved. The dilemma of AGP, in and out of office twice over the last two decades, highlights strikingly both these contradictions (Prabhakara 2004).

The AGP's inability to adopt a clear-cut stand on electoral alliance strategies since its emergence as a political force in Assam is a clear failure on its part. In successive polls, the party joined hands with different parties, including the Left and the BJP, to the detriment of its own image as a regional party with a highly variegated multi-ethnic electoral base. The lack of ideology, failure to address the basic issues on which party was formed, along with opportunism and factionalism within the party were some of the factors that contributed to the defeat of the AGP in the elections. The ruling AGP faced the test of its popularity in the mid-term Lok Sabha elections held in 1998. In the 2001 assembly elections, the AGP government was voted out unceremoniously in favour of Congress led by Tarun Gogoi. The AGP, therefore, needs a total makeover, a change of ideology and also a complete overhaul in its leadership and its organization base. It is to be remembered that the structural reasons that produced regional parties in Assam have not totally disappeared; rather these may be present in some areas even more intensely lying in dormant state.

This chapter reflects on the changing nature of politics in the state with the emergence of a new regional party, that is, the AGP. In the next chapter, we explore the causes for the comeback of Congress in the state.

REFERENCES

Barma, A. 1996. 'Playing Ethnic Politics'. *Frontline*, 17 May.

Barua, Apurba, and Sandhya Goswami. 1999. 'Fractured Identities: Politics in a Multi-ethnic State'. *Economic & Political Weekly* 34 (34–35, 21 August–3 September): 2492–2501.

Baruah, Joydeep. 2009. 'Egotistic Alliance sans Real Politics'. *The Assam Tribune*, May 24.

Choudhury, K. 2001. 'An Alliance of Convenience'. *Frontline*, 27 April.

Dasgupta, Jyotirindra. 1998. 'Community, Authenticity and Autonomy: Insurgency and Institutional Development in India's North-East'. In *Community Conflicts and the State in India*, edited by Amrita Basu and Atul Kohli. New York: Oxford University Press.

Dutta, Arup Kumar. 2011. 'When Reality Bites'. *The Assam Tribune*, 16 July.

Goswami, Manoronjan. 2009. 'A Wake Up Call for AGP'. *The Assam Tribune*, 23 May.

Goswami, Sandhya. 1998. 'Lok Sabha Election Results in Assam: An Analysis'. *The Assam Tribune*, 20 March.

Goswami, Sandhya. 2001a. 'Ethnic Conflict in Assam'. *The Indian Journal of Political Science* 6 (1, March): 123–137.

———. 2001b. 'Assam: Changing Electoral Trends'. *Economic & Political Weekly* 36 (12–18 May): 12–18.

———. 2003a. 'Assam Multiple Realignments and Fragmentation of Party System'. *Journal of Indian School of Political Economy* 15 (1, 2 January): 220–247.

———. 2003b. 'Vote against Mis-governance, Reflections on a By-election'. *Economic & Political Weekly* 38 (14, 5 April): 5–11.

Goswami, Sandhya. 2004. 'Assam Mixed Verdict'. *Economic & Political Weekly* 39 (51, December): 5523–5526.

———. 2006. 'Democracy and Governance in Assam'. *Indian Journal of Politics* 40 (4, October–December): 125–150.

———. 2009. 'Assam: A Fractured Verdict'. *Economic & Political Weekly* 14 (39): 159–163.

———. 2011. 'Mandate for Peace in Assam'. *Economic & Political Weekly* 46 (23, 4–10 June): 20–22.

———. 2011. 'Congress's Assets in Assam'. *The Indian Express*, 17 May.

———. 2013. 'Asom Gana Parishad: Rise and Prospects'. In *Handbook of Politics in Indian States: Regions, Parties and Economic Reforms*, edited by Sudha Pai, 197–211. New Delhi: Oxford University Press.

Goswami, Sandhya, and S. Sharma. 1993. 'Voting Pattern in 1991 Assam Assembly Election: An Analysis'. *Teaching Politics* 20 (3).

Hazarika, Sanjay. 1994. *Strangers of the Mist*. New Delhi: Penguin.

India Today, 'Victory of Asom Gana Parishad ushers in new era of hope and change in Assam', 15 January 1986.

Kohli, Atul. 1996. 'The Challenges Ahead'. *India Today*, 15 June.

Mahanta, Nani Gopal. 2013. *Confronting the State: ULFA's Quest for Sovereignty*. New Delhi: SAGE Publications.

Misra, Udayon. 1990a. 'Twilight of Asom Gana Parishad'. *Economic & Political Weekly* 25 (5): 247–248.

———. 1990b. 'The Assam Gana Parishad: Shedding Its Regional Image'. *N E Politics* 1 (2): 5–8.

———. 2006. 'Assam: New Equations and Uneasy Alliances'. *Economic & Political Weekly* 41 (23, 10–16 June): 2291–2293.

Palshikar, Suhas. 2015, 9 May. 'Congress in the Times of the Post Congress Era'. *Economic & Political Weekly* 50 (19): 39–46.

Pani, N. 1996. 'Regional Nationalism Challenge to National Parties'. *The Times of India*, 16 May.

Prabhakara, M. S. 2004. 'From Agitation to Governance'. *Frontline* 21 (10–23 April).

Roy, Ramashray, Sujata Miri, and Sandhya Goswami. 1997. *Northeast India: Development, Communalism and Insurgency*. New Delhi: Anshah Publishing House.

Roy, Tapas. 1996. 'AGP Come Back in Assam'. *Frontline*, 31 May.

Sharma, Manorama, and Apurba Barua. 1985. 'Who Is the Gana? An Analysis of the AGP Manifesto from Assam Elections 1985'. *North East Quarterly* 2 (January–March): 21–28.

———. 1987. 'Promises to Keep: An Analysis of the AGP Manifesto'. *North East Quarterly* 2 (2).

Yadav, Yogendra. 2001. 'On Predictable Lines'. *Frontline*, 8 June.

———. 2009. 'How India Voted'. *The Hindu*, 26 May.

Yadav, Yogendra, and Sanjay Kumar. 2006. 'Assembly Elections 2006: An Election Too Close to Call'. *The Hindu*, 9 April.

Recovery of Congress

The Congress's recovery in Assam began in the late 90s as in a few other states in India. With it the notion about national parties losing their relevance with the rise of regional party in Assam seemed to have proved wrong. The Congress party made a remarkable come-back from 1998 till 2014 in both Lok Sabha and assembly elections. On the other hand, the BJP led National Democratic Alliance (NDA) formed its government at the centre for the first time in 1998. The Congress party, no doubt, faced a great challenge at the national level with the rise of BJP as an alternate party. The Congress party's victory in the state was not unexpected as it has a wide support base across the state. But the emergence of BJP as the main Opposition party in the state sidelining the regional party AGP, whose leaders at one time spearheaded the Assam Movement, could not win even a single seats in the two consecutive elections (Srikanth 2000) was definitely an important point for reflection.

The pluralist character of the Congress party may have contributed to regain its popularity in the state. The Congress party could con-solidate its position not only in Lok Sabha elections, but also in the state for three consecutive terms. In fact, the assembly elections 2011 made a political history. The incumbent Congress government headed by Tarun Gogoi, like that of his predecessor Bimola Prasad Chaliha, managed to win a third time, a rare achievement for any political party in contemporary Indian politics where 'anti-incumbency' has become the norm (Goswami 2011b). Even in the Lok Sabha elections, the party could improve its position in all four elections from 1998 to 2009 (Tables 5.1 and 5.2). Although the party is back in power in the state, the Congress is no longer an umbrella organization that

Table 5.1 *Lok Sabha Elections in Assam: 1998–2009*

Political Party	1998		1999		2004		2009	
	Seat Secured	Votes Polled	Seat Secured	Votes Polled	Seat Secured	Votes Polled	Seat Secured	Votes Polled
Congress	10	39.00	10	38.42	9	35.07	7	34.89
AGP	–	12.70	0	11.09	2	20.00	1	14.60
BJP	1	24.50	2	29.84	3[a]	30.80	4	16.21
CPI	–	1.00	–	0.60	–	1.66	–	0.92
CPM	–	3.30	–	–	–	0.66	–	0.70
ASDC	1	2.20	1	–	–	0.98	–	–
UMF	1	4.30	–	–	0	0.62	–	–
JD	–	–	–	–	–	1.21	–	–
AIUDF	–	–	–	–	–	–	1	16.10
BPPF	–	–	–	–	–	–	1	5.41
IND	1	9.50	1	9.40	1	–	–	–
Others	1	5.60	–	5.80	1	13.41	0	12.79

Source: CSDS Data Unit.

Note: [a] BJP+ includes one seat contested and won by an independent candidate supported by the BJP and one seat contested by the BJP's ally JD(U). In the 1999 Lok Sabha elections, one seat was won by the same independent candidate who was not supported by the BJP, and one by the CPI(ML).

Table 5.2 *Assembly Elections in Assam: 2001–2011*

Political Party	2001		2006		2011	
	Seat Secured	*Votes Polled*	*Seat Secured*	*Votes Polled*	*Seat Secured*	*Votes Polled*
Congress	70	39.75	53	31.00	78	39.38
AGP	20	20.10	24	20.39	10	16.30
AGP(P)	–	–	1	3.39	–	–
BJP	8	9.30	10	11.98	5	11.50
AIUDF	–	–	10	16.12	18	12.60
BPPF	–	–	11	3.72	12	6.10
IND	19	19.50	22	9.71	–	–
Others	2	3.70	–	–	3	14.20

Source: CSDS Data Unit.

accommodates the various ethnicities and communities in the state (Goswami 2012). The decline of Congress dominance was caused by the emergence of multipolar party competition and the assertion and realignment of ethnic identities. Its performance remains insipid and capacity to attract new coalition partners remain limited. The inability on the part of the Congress to accommodate the social churning that took place since the 1980s must have contributed to its decline. Essentially, Congress's decline is also due to the result of paradigmatic changes in the polity, economy and society. Besides, after 1991, more vigorously emerged the process of liberalization and reforms with emphasis on withdrawal of state, entry of market and linkage of global capital as globalization set in.

RETURN OF CONGRESS IN LOK SABHA ELECTIONS (1998, 1999, 2004 AND 2019)

A complete reversal of the electoral reality unfolded in the state since 1998. This election was a reminder to the party in power in the state that even an unlettered electorate can and will have recourse to retributive justice if necessary. This election saw the virtual eclipse of the AGP for its failure to fulfil election-eve promises. The state has come out strongly in favour of the Congress again. Certain underlying factors were responsible for such an outcome. The situation that prevailed in the state before the Lok Sabha elections was not favourable to the party in power in the state. Contrary to popular expectations of a party opposed to state terrorism (because of its own experiences that led to its formation and commitment made in the election manifesto), the AGP-led government imposed repressive measures, in the shape of a unified command, similar in form and content to those followed by the Congress earlier. This led to the alienation of the Assamese middle class from the AGP. The performance of the government was also so inept that even a normal obligation like payment of salaries to employees, including schoolteachers, release of funds for institutions of higher learning such as universities could not be fulfilled. The bitter confrontation of the government with the major teahouses like the Tatas over the issue of harbouring extremists had also reflected the immaturity on the part of the government. The attempts of the tea groups to placate the ultras was understandable, particularly in view of the growing power of the extremist groups in the state during the preceding few years, but the government's failure to provide security to the industry, which was so vital to its economy, definitely eroded its credibility. This confrontation with the tea lobby drained a lot of energy and time, when vital problems such as extremist violence, ethnic conflicts and infiltration plagued the state. The letter of credit (LoC) scandal regarding illegal withdrawal of more than hundreds of crores of rupees from the government treasury in connection with the supply of fodder to the veterinary department, involving several ministers of the earlier government as well as the incumbent ministry including its chief minister together with a host of government officials, turned out to be one of the major scandals that rocked the state and provided the Opposition a powerful plank in the election campaign against the AGP. The extremists' call to the people to keep away from electoral process had further added to the uncertainty and confusion prevailed in the state. To make matters worse, the killing of a close aide of AGP president, in Nagaon by ULFA, instilled fear among the workers of political parties. ULFA's call to the people to boycott the polls came as a surprise as the extremist outfit in the earlier elections had not given such an ultimatum to the masses. In fact, the 1991 and 1996 polls had passed off without interference with the fundamental rights of the people. The state of affairs was further complicated for the AGP by the fact that unlike in 1996, smaller ethnic and religious parties such as ASDC, PDF and UMF did not join hands with AGP in this election. The coming together of the tribal groups such as the ASDC, Mishing Mimang Kebang Autonomous Demand Struggling Front and the Karbi Anglong unit of the CPI(Marxist–Leninist)—CPI(ML)—under the banner of Assam People's Front (APF) was significant for the political process in Assam. The AGP stood alienated from the tribal electorate. Another problem the party faced was factional politics within it, which led to the exit of Bhrigu Kumar Phukan, the former AASU general secretary and the most important leader of Assam Movement who played an important role in the formation of Assam Jatiya Parishad.

The problems of insurgency, corruption, ethnic identity, repeal of IMDT Act and stability constituted the main poll plank for electoral propaganda in the 1998 elections. The Congress party's campaign concentrated on the 'stability plank'. In a separate mani-festo on Assam, the party had promised to undertake and execute certain schemes like preparing a master plan for flood control in the Brahmaputra and Barak Valleys. It also favoured a peaceful solution to the burning insurgency problem in the state. Further, it pleaded for shifting the Oil India and tea garden headquarters to the state. In the economic front, the manifesto called for a separate economic policy for the northeastern region in order to create avenues of employment for the unemployed youth. Further, it emphasized on the preparation of a correct voters list. The BJP, on the other hand, incorporated a section on 'North East' in its manifesto, where it promised to repeal the IMDT Act and strengthen the existing immi-gration laws and rules and enact new ones to make illegal infiltration difficult and deny the extension of benefits of citizenship to such entrants. To be in tune with the aspirations generated by the 'Assam Movement' over the foreigners' issue, the party promised to maintain a National Registrar of Citizens. The party also promised a plan to deal with the unabated infiltration from across the border, apparently with an eye on the electorate in Assam. The main plank of the United Front campaign was the development of Assam. The APF, a combine of ASDC, Autonomy Demand Struggling Forum (ADSF) and CPI(ML), promised to continue with its relentless efforts to form a strong regional force to fight the corrupt AGP, Congress (I) and BJP in the state. Asom Jatiya Sanmilan (AJS) in its manifesto focused on the issues of correct voters list up to year 2000, repeal of IMDT Act, solution of the unemployment problem, flood control and a corruption-free state. The ethnic issue in fact remained the focal point of ASDC manifesto. Thus corruption, political autonomy and cultural identity of smaller communities, state repression, immigration and development remained major issues in the election campaign. But corruption and ethnic identity seemed to overshadow all other issues.

The 1998 Lok Sabha elections were particularly significant as they were held in the midst of a call by militant organizations, namely the ULFA and Bodo extremists, for boycott of elections. As a consequence, voter turnout remained low particularly in the Assamese-dominated constituencies of the state (General Election Report 1998). That electioneering was on a very low key was also evident from the data of post-poll survey conducted by CSDS. The survey indicates low intensity of canvassing as well as voters' participation in poll campaign. The poll boycott call was, however, instrumental in leaning the balance in favour of the Congress party that capitalized on its known pockets of influence, particularly among the minorities and tea garden communities of the state (Goswami 1998). While the electoral base of the Congress was shrinking and eroding in many states in India, the party appeared to have been able to maintain part of its electoral base in the state. The Congress party consolidated its position, and polled 38.9 per cent votes and gained 10 seats and its ally, while UMF won one seat. AGP and its allies, CPI(M) and CPI, contested on 12 seats but failed to retain even one of the five seats it held in the last election. Smaller parties reflecting the ethnic and religious identities, namely ASDC and UMF, supported by Congress and an independent candidate supported by ABSU could retain one seat each.

CHANGING PATTERN OF SUPPORT BASE

A changing pattern of support base of the Congress party was noticed in the 1998 elections. The post-poll survey revealed that the support base of the Congress among the Muslims went up to 75.6 per cent as against 50 per cent in 1996, while support for the BJP among Muslims remained unchanged. The change in acceptance of BJP is shown by substantial gains in support from groups that had previously shunned it, namely the SCs. The BJP also increased its base among the STs and OBCs. The increase in its vote base among the SCs and STs came at the cost of the AGP. The CSDS post-poll survey reveals that the community-wise pattern of voting by age, gender and class remained similar to what was noticed in the 1996 elections despite a severe shift in the voting turnout for different parties. The Congress gained in all the sections and the AGP lost almost everywhere, but in relative terms the relationship did not change much. Clearly, the disenchantment with AGP affected women more than men. In class terms, the Congress maintained a classical subaltern profile—the lower the educational opportunity, the higher the vote for the Congress.

REGION-WISE ANALYSIS

For region wise analysis, the assembly constituencies of Assam have been divided into four broad categories: (a) those with the dominance of immigrants, (b) those where the STs are numerically preponderant, (c) those seats of Upper Assam dominated by tea garden community and (d) the remaining seats that are dominated by the dominant Asomiya community. The category-wise analysis of this election shows that the phenomenon of immigrant Muslim votes to the Congress and caste Hindu votes to BJP was apparent in the Lok Sabha elections. The Congress could retain Dibrugarh and Jorhat tea garden labour-dominated Lok Sabha seats. The BJP was also successful to a great extent to find a foothold in this region. It increased its base among the tea community at the cost of AGP. But the fact remains that events preceding the elections deflected their electoral preference away from the AGP and closer to the Congress. Moreover, during the last decades or so quite a few new political leaders emerged among the tea communities, several of whom occupied very responsible positions in the Congress ministry and enjoyed considerable political clout. No such leader had emerged among the supporters of other political parties including AGP. Even the students' leaders of the tea community who were parts of the Assam movement shifted ground. INTUC, the oldest labour organization having allegiance to Congress, contributed significantly in affecting the swing towards the Congress.

The results of the immigrant-dominant constituencies also went in favour of Congress. Interestingly, loyalty of a sizeable portion of minority Muslims who sided with AGP and allies in the last election shifted to Congress this time. The Congress retained all the seats in these areas by polling high percentages of votes. The major reason for this change might have been the apprehension in the minds of minority community that in the event of BJP forming the government at the Centre it would certainly repeal the IMDT Act, which was to prove detrimental to the interests of immigrant religious minority. Further, the minorities seemed to have lost their trust in AGP for its mysterious silence over the immigration issue, particularly when AASU urged the Centre and the state government to delete the names of those voters marked as 'doubtful' in the electoral roll published in 1997 and to repeal the IMDT Act. It was apparent from the election results that the religious minorities rallied on the side of the Congress and the immigrant linguistic Hindu minority as well as a small portion of indigenous people supported the BJP. But the shift of the minority support was to be seen in the context of the position of the UMF. Electoral alliance with UMF in Barpeta constituency helped the Congress to enhance its position. UMF which could poll only 26.7 per cent of votes in the 1996 elections was catapulted to a high of 58.64 per cent of votes in this election. Hindu polarization in Assam invariably seemed to have consolidated the Muslim voters into a more organized community (Dutta 1998).

Tribal-dominant constituencies indicated the existing assertive behaviour of the tribal electorate in support of their ethnic identity. The tribals have perpetually experienced the problem of land alienation, poverty, indebtedness, severe unemployment, economic exploitation and cultural exploitation. Therefore, the emerging tribal movements started asserting their views on demands like creation of Udayachal, Bodoland and an autonomous tribal state in the hills from the 1991 elections onwards. In the Karbi-dominated autonomous parliamentary constituency, the ASDC candidate Jayanta Rongpi was elected to Parliament for the fourth consecutive term and the ASDC's margin over Congress was quite high. The BJP increased its vote share in these areas from 3.06 per cent in 1996 to 12.00 per cent in 1998. In the Bodo areas, however, the winning margins were not high as no dominant Bodo leader emerged. Sansuma Khunggur Bwiswmuthiary, backed by ABSU, won the election by polling 25.5 per cent of total votes, while Congress candidate Premsingh Brahma, former militant Bodo leader, could poll only 11.8 per cent of votes. Significantly, vote share of AGP candidate went down as the party could poll only 6.3 per cent of votes, while BJP's vote share remained at 15.3 per cent. The election results in these areas clearly reflect the ethnic polarization as well as ethnic accommodation.

PRE-ELECTION SCENARIO 1999

Another Lok Sabha election came sooner than anyone expected. The BJP's short-lived rule at the Centre began to affect political agenda of the state. With the election drawing nearer certain disquieting developments began to agitate public mind. A spate of news about Pakistani Inter Service Intelligence (ISI) conspiracies and intrigues in Assam have appeared in local newspapers. News about the possible links between the ISI and fundamentalists forces in the media just before the elections caused widespread unease and fear among the Muslim communities. The state machinery was in fact responsible for spreading such rumours. Even the Chief Minister himself made such a statement as Madrasas being the hotbed of ISI intrigues in Assam.

In the meantime, the decision of the Assam Jatiyatabadi Yuba Parishad, to form a new regional party called All Assam Gana Sangram Parishad added a new dimension to the regional political scenario.

The aim of the proposed party to stand as a political alternative to uphold and rejuvenate regionalism in the state was a direct challenge to the ruling AGP. The formation of an alternative regional party is likely to be crucial in deciding the fortunes of regional forces, keeping in view the highly polarized demographic pattern in the state. However, this time the AGP benefited from the fact that the AASU, a main stay of Asomiya regional sentiments decided not to oppose the poll, in sharp contrast to the 1998 elections when the AASU had called a 23-hour bandh to protest against holding of polls, as names of foreigners were not deleted from the electoral rolls. Moreover, the president of the organization relinquished his post and joined the AGP to become its candidate for the Lakhimpur constituency. The split within the UMF, an ally of the Congress, affected the electoral prospect of the Congress. One section led by the Hafiz faction merged with Nationalist Congress Party (NCP) and another faction led by Osmani merged with the Congress before the elections in its bid to solve the problem of minorities. However, with Jamiat Ulema-e-Hind's decision to support the Congress (I) all over the country, the Congress (I) was hopeful of retaining substantial support of the religious minority voters.

ROLE OF INSURGENT GROUPS IN ELECTIONS

The insurgent groups have been playing a dominant role in influencing the democratic process in the state. The ULFA's role in the 1998 polls came under scanner following its active campaign against the ruling AGP through coercion, intimidation and even murder of the active workers and district-level AGP leaders of the ruling party AGP. This anti-democratic campaign of the banned outfit resulted in the staying away of large segments of the electorate from the polls in 1998. With the fear psychosis grip in large areas of the Brahmaputra Valley on account of the grave threat from the banned outfit, the exercise of franchise by the people was severely affected. However, in the 1999 elections, the same threat from misguided elements remained in parts of the Brahmaputra Valley but with a difference. This time the ULFA had vowed to make this election a bloody one. But the situation in the state had by then undergone a see-saw change due to the assertion of the people against extremist violence. Despite bandh calls and some incidents of violence, like the murder of the BJP candidate from Dhubri and the gunning down of three AGP supporters and police personnel, the people showed that their voice cannot be silenced and intimidated. People in countryside turned out in large numbers to cast their votes. In Nalbari district, for example, which is considered to be a hotbed of insurgent activities, the polling was peaceful and 48 per cent voters exercised their franchise. Voters silently registered their conscious defiance of the ULFA's ban on polls and this included even members of ULFA leaders' families.

The mid-term poll did not enthuse the electorate in Assam. The fractured polity confronted by many problems, including insurgency and insurgency-related ethnic conflicts along with growing unemployment, seemed to see very little light even in the most vital democratic exercise. Apart from a couple of posters and graffiti put up by parties like the Congress, AGP and BJP, no other visible election campaign was witnessed in the state. Election fever was significantly in a low ebb this time. There were no big rallies, nor processions or proper campaigning. No issue seemed to have emerged as crucial, even though implications of insurgency with their impact on the people emerged as a major issue on the agenda of the electorate. It appears political parties tried to get votes by levelling charges and accusations against each other. The euphoria over Kargil issue did work in some parts of Assam. The CSDS survey showed that out of the respondents who were satisfied with the government's action and who said Kargil had influenced their vote, there was a strong swing towards the BJP. However, since on the balance there were more people who were satisfied than dissatisfied with the central government's action in Kargil, the BJP made a net gain out of the Kargil conflict. Illegal migration of people from the neighbouring Bangladesh was no longer the main poll plank of any of the political parties of the state. AGP, which was formed as a fallout of Assam Movement for the detection and deportation of foreigners from Assam, also sought to undermine the issue, apparently for the fear of losing immigrants votes. Their manifesto only said that the foreigners living in the state should be deported as per the provisions of the

Assam Accord and the erection of the barbed wire fencing along the international border should be completed soon. Significantly, the Congress promised to effectively check illegal infiltration a major contentious issue of the region and to establish border trade routes at selected location along the international border. However, the Assam State Committee of the BJP made illegal migration one of its main planks, but the manifesto of the NDA remained silent on the issue The NDA manifesto said that the Alliance would maintain territorial integrity of the North Eastern region and would deal with the security related problems. The NCP in Assam seemed to have moved according to its own strategy. In a separate region-specific manifesto NCP promised to treat the Northeast as a special develop-mental zone. Its game plan seemed to have designed to boost BJP's support so as to weaken the Congress. The Left parties maintained a low profile. The creation of a separate state of Bodoland seemed to be the main election plank of the candidates supported by the ethnic-based parties in the Bodo area like the ABSU and the Bodo People's Action Committee (BPAC).

THE LOK SABHA ELECTION VERDICT, 1999

The Lok Sabha election in Assam in 1999 was more or less a replica of the 1998 Lok Sabha election with seemingly minor and yet very significant shift in the power balance. The verdict of the electorate was clearly a reflection of the electorate's disillusionment with AGP, the torchbearer of regional politics in the state. The split before the elections not only divided the committed regional vote between AGP and the newly formed parties like Asom Gana Sangram but also eroded the credibility of a party torn apart by personality clashes.

The Congress seemed to have marginally capitalized on the split in the AGP's vote bank, yet its support base had not significantly increased. Undoubtedly, the process of formation of regional politics has been marked by ebb and flows, thereby keeping alive the hopes and prospects of the national parties like Congress and BJP. The strength and weakness of the Congress and BJP appeared to be a function of aggregation or disaggregation of regional political parties based on various ethnic, cultural and regional issues.

The Congress party appeared to have consolidated the gain it made in the 1998 election. The party polled 38.42 per cent of votes and won 11 seats, while only one of its candidates from tribal-dominant constituency lost security deposit. The significant development of this election was that the BJP emerged as an important electoral force. The party not only increased its vote share to 29.84 per cent but also expanded its support base throughout Assam. The BJP's success could be attributed mainly to the Kargil issue and also its promise to repeal the IMDT Act, thereby allaying the fear of the indigenous Assamese of being wiped out. Further, dissatisfaction and disenchantment with the ruling party had alienated the people, mainly the urban middle class. Smaller parties like ASDC in alliance with CPI (ML) and an independent candidate supported by ABSU could retain one seat each. On the whole, the mandate was against the AGP-led alliance and therefore indicative of decline of the AGP's support base among the Muslim, SC and ST communities. The analysis of post-poll survey clearly reveals that the significant shift of the ST and Muslims votes to Congress and the caste Hindu votes to BJP led to the debacle of AGP in the election (Table 5.3).

CONSTITUENCY-WISE VOTING PATTERN

The voting pattern in constituencies dominated by communities such as tea-tribes, immigrant Muslims and STs reflects an interesting trend (Table 5.3). A significant shift of tea garden community and immigrant Muslim votes to the Congress and caste Hindu votes to BJP has led to the AGP's set back in this Lok Sabha election. The Congress could retain the Jorhat and Dibrugarh tea garden-dominated constituencies by polling 48.30 per cent and 48.57 per cent of votes, respectively. The BJP also made considerable inroads into the tea garden vote bank, traditionally considered a Congress bastion. The party had polled 32 to 36 per cent votes in these constituencies. The confrontation and bitterness that developed between AGP and the few major teahouses might have a multiplying effect on the entire tea community deflecting their electoral preferences away from the party and closer to the Congress. Moreover, during the last decades, quite a few new political leaders have emerged among the tea communities, several of whom

Table 5.3 *Who Voted for Whom: 1996–1999 Lok Sabha Elections*

Community	1996			1998			1999		
	INC	BJP	AGP	INC	BJP	AGP	INC	BJP	AGP
Scheduled Caste	22.1	11.1	66.7	50.0	50.0	0.0	14.0	14.0	0
Scheduled Tribe	38.1	19.0	33.3	25.0	37.5	25.0	28.6	9.3	5.0
Other Backward Classes	27.1	27.1	44.7	45.2	38.7	14.0	28.4	46.5	75.0
Others	39.4	12.8	47.9	68.1	12.1	8.8	0	23.3	10.0
Hindus	23.4	28.9	46.1	41.2	42.9	13.4	–	–	–
Muslims	50.0	2.7	47.3	75.6	2.6	9.0	38.8	4.7	10.0
Male	36.1	17.2	44.3	57.4	24.3	12.0	55.1	62.8	67.6
Female	29.9	21.8	48.2	51.4	39.1	10.8	44.9	37.2	32.5

Source: Based on Assam sample of the post-poll survey of the NES conducted by CSDS.

occupied responsible positions in the Congress ministry and enjoyed considerable political clout.

The Muslim population by and large plays a decisive role in the Assam elections and is becoming more and more relevant in electoral terms because of its increasing numbers. The growth rates of the population in immigrant-dominated constituencies such as Dhubri (70.45%), Barpeta (56.07%), Goalpara (50.18%) and Hailakandi (55.42%)[1] clearly reflect this fact. The INC, had enjoyed an unflinching support from the community since Independence, except during the 1985 and 1996 elections, when a split in the Muslim vote was inevitable due to the emergence of the significance held by regional, ethnic and cultural-based parties in state politics. Therefore, terms such as division and polarization with regard to Muslim votes have a special relevance in the context of Assam's politics even at the threshold of the 21st century. However, Hindu polarization in Assam as an anti-pole to Muslim polarization did not take place in any past election. But as an exception and belying all speculations, a Hindu polarization too was noticed in the 1999 elections (Dutta 1998). The results in immigrant-dominant constituencies such as Barpeta, Mangaldoi and Dhubri went in favour of the Congress. The election results of Nagaon constituency, however, due to a high percentage of polling (over 100,000 more voters cast votes compared to the 1998 elections) went in favour of the BJP. The vote share of BJP has increased while not much change was noticed in the voting percentage of the AGP. It is apparent from the election results that the religious minority rallied on the side of the Congress and the immigrant Hindu polarization in Assam invariably consolidated the Muslim votes in a more organized way. The rise of the BJP in religious minority-dominant constituencies, namely Dhubri, Nagaon and Barpeta, has only helped parties like the Congress and UMF (Barua and Goswami 1999).

The Congress appeared be weak in tribal belts. High turnout of voters in these constituencies in the last few elections indicates prevailing assertive behaviour of the tribal votes in support of their

---

[1] For further details, see Census of India 1991.

ethnic identity. The tribals have perpetually experienced the problems of land alienation, poverty, indebtedness, severe unemployment and economic and cultural exploitation. The Assamese middle-class's insistence on a dominantly Assamese linguistic identity for the state and the support given to this notion by the ruling party went a long way in alienating first the hill tribes and then the plain tribes. It was evident that the Assamese middle-class leadership, preoccupied as it was with the struggle to establish Assamese hegemony, had failed to respond to the growing sense of insecurity in the tribal mind. As a result, this sense of alienation came to be expressed in the growth of different tribal organizations which started demanding political power and social justice (Misra 1989). Therefore, the emerging tribal movements have started asserting their views in favour of their demands, namely the creation of Udayachal, Bodoland and an autonomous tribal state. Thus, the election results in the constituencies dominated by tribal groups (Kokrajhar and Autonomous Districts) clearly reflected an emerging trend of ethnic polarization and accommodation.

RETURN OF THE CONGRESS
IN ASSEMBLY ELECTIONS 2001

The one-sided verdict of the Lok Sabha elections had set the stage for the forthcoming state assembly elections held on 10 May 2001 (Table 5.4). The decline of electoral support for the ruling party AGP and a corresponding increase in Congress strength became clear. AGP's popularity had declined on account of its government's poor performance. The party had not taken care to restrain its rapacity and share the trials and tribulations of the people. There were allegations of its involvement in secret killings as well as rampant corruption. On the eve of the declaration of the poll schedule, the AGP announced several schemes, notably the chief minister's self-employment scheme, appointment of teachers under Operation Blackboard, appointment to fill up the vacant posts in the Assam Electricity Board, etc. These schemes were apparently aimed at mustering the support of the unemployed youth and their family members in the assembly elections. All these deeds, however, failed to make a favourable impression on the

Table 5.4 *Community-wise Support Base: 2001 Assembly Elections*

Community	INC	BJP	AGP	Others
Kayastha	21.4	14.3	18.6	45.7
Other Upper Castes	32.2	16.8	21.7	29.4
Upper OBCs	34.8	13.6	20.5	31.1
Lower OBCs	48.6	24.3	10.0	17.1
Rajbanshis	17.9	3.6	50.0	28.6
Other SCs	50.5	10.3	17.5	21.6
Bodo	4.4	4.4	29.4	61,8
Miri	36.1	–	16.7	47.2
Other STs	30.8	10.3	22.4	36.4
Muslims	58.8	1.6	13.9	25.7
Others	62.8	7.0	8.1	22.1

Source: Assam Assembly election study, 2001, post-poll survey carried out by CSDS with the author as the state coordinator.

Note: A stratified random sample of 1,236 electors was selected from 24 assembly constituencies. The respondents were approached the day after polling (or within a few days, but before the counting of votes), given a dummy ballot paper of their constituency and asked to indicate the candidate they had voted for. The reported voting pattern has been weighted here by the actual vote share of the leading parties at the state level.

public. The writing was on the wall for everyone to read. As one of the leading newspapers commented:

> Schemes aimed at public welfare are welcome, but they cannot be an end in themselves. What is of utmost importance is their proper implementation. It is here that the AGP government has not proved its competence. Undeserving persons were appointed as teachers who cannot play an effective role in improving the quality of education. Similar anomalies are said to have crept into the process of the implementation of their public welfare scheme. What further appears to have alienated the people from the AGP is the rampant corruption prevailing at all levels of the government. The government was expected to take steps that will eliminate corrupt practices in the government departments but sadly enough, nothing concrete was done. This has inevitably lowered the image of AGP in public estimation. Further the government has not done noteworthy in the direction of bringing an

end to the ULFA–SULFA conflict that has silenced many precious lives. It looks as if the AGP wants to keep this conflict alive for serving its political purposes. (*The North East Times*, 30 March 2001)

The ULFA indulged in large-scale violence in the run-up to the election. Political violence and vengeance in the state had taken away many precious lives untimely. For example, the rebels had killed as many as 1,548 people, including 333 security personnel, in Assam between 1997 and 2000. In 2000, in separate attacks between October and December, a total of 109 Hindi-speaking people had been massacred by armed militants in different parts of Assam (Hussain 2001). However, there was revulsion in the state against violence. People in thousands took to the streets to denounce the violence by militants. This kind of mass protest was a clear indication of people's displeasure with the functioning of the government.

ALLIANCE FORMATION

The election scenario in Assam took a significant turn with the decision of the AGP and BJP leadership to forge an alliance in spite of the strong opposition from the state units of both the parties. The AGP was doubtful if it could win on its own. Therefore, it gravitated towards this arrangement of convenience (Chaudhari 2001). The understanding between the two brought about a new equation in the electoral politics of the state. The poll-alliance issue flared up anger, dissatisfaction and intensive conflict among the BJP rank and the file. The BJP youth leaders held big rallies at the state BJP head office in Guwahati to protest against the alliance decision. For several days in succession the head office of the BJP's Assam unit at Guwahati came under attack of the disgruntled elements of the party. In the case of AGP, the resentment was less violent and subdued. The state BJP leaders, though faction-ridden, were at least in touch with grassroots cadres. The decision about the alliance had been taken over their heads and behind their backs by the national party set-up. This was hardly a welcome sign for successful working of democracy and effective intraparty solidarity. A senior BJP leader, Hiranya Bhattacharyya, resigned from the party and floated a new party called Asom BJP. He even decided to put up

60 candidates in the election. The 'friendly' contests between the AGP and BJP in 10 constituencies further fuelled controversy.

By aligning itself with the BJP, AGP lost three of its former allies—the CPI, CPM and the United People's Party (UPP). The UPP, representing the minority interests, joined hands with the Samajwadi Party (SP). The AGP–BJP alliance, however, had managed to come to an understanding with the ABSU and the Haliram Terang faction of the ASDC. There were doubts in the public mind as to how much influence these groups would wield in their troubled and divided communities. Although the ABSU still matters most in Bodo politics, the AGP would have been in a more advantageous position if it had forged an alliance with the UMF. In that case, a significant segment of Muslims would have propped up the party's poll prospects. The Congress party also became wise to the political fragmentation and came to an understanding with the UMF. In the past elections, the Congress party had not felt the need for election alliance or adjustments as the Opposition had never presented a real threat.

This election also witnessed a third front. The NCP had come to an understanding with seven smaller parties: Asom Gana Sangram Parishad (AGSP), Purbanchaliya Lok Parishad (PLP), AJS, Janata Dal (JD; Secular), RCPI, and Asom Labour Party (ALP). They formed a regional democratic alliance as an alternative to the Congress and AGP–BJP partnership. Although 40 political parties, including national ones, took part in the election and 914 candidates filed nomination papers, the main contenders were the Congress and AGP–BJP alliance.

Seat adjustments, regrouping and internal squabbles within the parties for the tickets appeared to be of more concern to parties than issues. Electors were seemingly not very enthusiastic about the election. Election campaign was confined to public meetings, poster-wars, banner display, wall writing with catchy slogans and mass rallies organized by different political party leaders. The campaign in this election was on a very low key as the issue of the alliance between the AGP and BJP and its after-effects had dominated the scene. Attendance was low even in the election meeting addressed by the prime minister.

The ULFA, through their pre-election activities induced fear among the supporters of the AGP and BJP combine (Goswami 2001). The campaign was marred by violence, revolved by and large around corruption, charges of nexus between the politicians and militants, illegal infiltration, scrapping the IMDT Act and other local issues. Like earlier elections, most of the parties this time also had promised to end insurgency and bring peace back, rid Assam of illegal foreign nationals, usher in economic growth, reduce unemployment and corruption and maintain the law and order situation. Secret killing too occupied the centre stage. The Congress manifesto committed itself to bringing to an end the problem of secret killings by giving priority and emphasis on talk with rebels and to initiate the process of political dialogue to solve the insurgency problem. Further, with regard to IMDT, it said, 'Congress will try its level best to foil any attempt to scrap the IMDT Act.' The failure of the AGP-led government to hold Panchayat elections during their tenure prompted the Congress to emphasize the issue. Holding Panchayat elections within a year was one of the major promises made by the party.

The AGP's electoral compulsions were clear. It was losing its core support to both Congress and the BJP as was evident from the 1998 and 1999 Lok Sabha elections. The Congress had already consolidated the Muslim and tea-garden votes. The AGP had to gain what it had lost of its core support to the Congress, its main enemy, and ally with the BJP to keep that support united. Therefore, IMDT Act and the foreigners' issue emerged as a major political plank for the allies. The AGP manifesto declared:

> Foreigners issue is a hangover in the process of development of the state and its security and safety. The demography is badly disturbed and the integrity of the state will be threatened if the foreigners' issue is not resolved once for all. AGP will leave no stone unturned to get the issue resolved with active co-operation of the Government of India. (Asom Gana Parishad 2001)

ELECTION OUTCOME

A resurgent Congress contesting against a discredited AGP however could not sweep the state; it won 71 seats, a clear majority but not the kind of majority that the prevailing situation would have taken place in any other state. Eventually, the surprise in the result was in the lack of a complete sweep in favour of the Congress. The AGP and its allies won 40 seats with a vote share of 36 per cent. But this big picture is somewhat misleading. It appears as though the Congress secured a large lead in terms of seats on the basis of a mere four-percentage-point lead over its rivals in votes. Actually, the vote shares of all candidates of the AGP-led alliance add up to 36 per cent only if we include even those seats where the partners fought each other. The AGP and the BJP together secured 29 per cent of the popular vote. Thus, on an average, for seats where the Congress faced the AGP–BJP combine, the Congress had a lead of 10 percentage points.

The verdict needs to be understood in its disaggregated patterns. The AGP and the BJP won 20 and 8, seats respectively. In terms of votes, AGP polled 20.1 per cent, while BJP polled 9.3 per cent of votes. The Left parties, once a force to reckon with, were wiped out. The weakening of ideological politics had marginalized the Left parties. Smaller parties like the ASDC(U), ABSU–BPAC, NCP (basically a regional outfit headed by Sarat Chandra Singha, under whose symbol Bhrigu Kumar Phukan's AJS contested the election), SP and Samata Party and independents together won 27 seats and polled over 30 per cent of votes. The AGP–BJP alliance brought immense gain to the ABSU–BPAC politics as these smaller formations managed to win 10 seats out of the 12 contested. Although this election was undoubtedly a victory for Congress, it was a boost to the smaller regional parties. This was the result of the fragmentation of the political space in Assam. The anti-foreigner movement led to Asomiya nationalism and also engendered various subregional and ethnic aspirations that found expression through smaller parties. The Congress won mostly at the expense of the let-downs caused by AGP and wrested all 40 seats that the AGP held earlier. Most of the gains came from the AGP's home turf of Lower Assam. However, the Congress did not quite sweep its stronghold of Upper Assam. It won 37 seats here, the same number of segments it led in the 1999 Lok Sabha elections and a gain of 14 over the last assembly elections. Unlike the 1991 elections, when most of the Congress seats came from Upper Assam, the Congress's performance in these two regions was balanced this time.

The AGP–BJP combine's prospects were adversely affected by the high levels of unpopularity of the Mahanta-led government, even among the AGP supporters. The AGP tried to avoid defeat by allying with the BJP, hoping to reap advantage of electoral arithmetic. But the alliance was strongly opposed and undermined by the workers of both the parties. Both the parties failed to persuade their supporters to vote for their alliance. However, this does not mean that the AGP would have won on its own in the absence of alliance. An analysis based on the survey conducted by CSDS suggests that if the two parties had contested separately, the AGP and BJP would have increased their vote shares 20–22 per cent and 9–15 per cent, respectively (Yadav 2001). But the logic of first-past-the-post system would have meant fewer seats for both the parties. Alliance or no alliance, the AGP faced a disaster.

The Congress managed a substantial increase in 2001 election, almost 10 per cent points, in its vote share compared to the previous election. In its traditional stronghold in the tea-growing areas, the party secured 10 percentage points more than its state average but won 20 out of 29 seats. The AGP–BJP alliance, on the other hand, could retain 8 seats with 35.8 per cent of votes, for its votes were concentrated in a few constituencies. The BJP seemed to have increased its support base among tea communities. The Congress established a clear lead in the Asomiya-dominated constituencies over the formidable AGP–BJP alliance. Although the survey results show that the AGP–BJP maintained an edge over the Congress among the Hindu upper caste respondents, this advantage of nearly 10 percentage points was wiped out among other communities, including the lower OBC's, SCs, STs other than the Bodos and 'others' representing the various ethnic minorities and smaller communities, thus resulting in an overall lead for the Congress. As expected, the BJP did well among the upper caste Hindus, but the AGP failed to secure any substantial lead in this section. In terms of caste, the AGP vote was fairly evenly distributed. It also managed a fair bit of the tribal vote, for its alliance with the Bodo formations.

A substantial portion of that lead seems to have come from the Muslim voters who constitute a little over one-fourth of the electorate and are known to have turned out in larger numbers. These are clear indications that the Congress regained Muslim support in this election. The AGP–BJP alliance failed to neutralize the apprehension and suspicion of religious minorities about the BJP's political ideology and agenda. The decision to go into alliance with the BJP must have cost the AGP a significant number of Muslim votes. The Congress won 8 of the 15 immigrant-dominated seats. But the effect was spread all over the state. The state-wide post-poll survey undertaken by the CSDS with a robust sample size of 1,236 voters confirms this reading. The survey data show that the Congress got an overwhelming 59 per cent of votes among the Muslim respondents, compared to only 14 for the AGP and negligible support for the BJP. A detailed analysis shows that the AGP–BJP counter mobilization also worked in 10 constituencies such as Hojai, Gauripur and Dhubri. It is apparent from the election results that the religious minorities rallied on the side of the Congress, and the immigrant Hindu minority as well as the indigenous people supported the BJP. Thereby, Hindu polarization in Assam invariably consolidates Muslim votes in a more organized way (Goswami 2003). This huge lead of about 40 percentage points among the Muslims may have made the vital difference between victory and defeat for the AGP. The election results proved again that any deviation from a policy of social inclusiveness cost the AGP very dearly.

Like the immigrant areas, the tribal belt constituencies also witnessed a turnout close to 80 per cent. This indicated the upsurge of the tribal electorate in support of their ethnic identity. The Congress did not get major chunk of the votes in these constituencies, but it forged ahead in Bodo areas to pick up eight seats with 30.3 per cent of votes, a big gain compared to the 1991 and 1996 assembly elections, when it could win only one seat in these areas. As many as 40 per cent votes went to independent candidates in the tribal seats. These included the ABSU–BPAC candidates in the Bodo areas who were allied to the AGP but contested as independents. The AGP also did a little better in these seats due to tribal allies. The survey results support these reading. The Congress was virtually blanked among the Bodos, while it got some support among the Miris and other tribal groups. It is clear that but for support among the tribal groups, the

AGP could have suffered a much worse electoral performance. Besides its unpopularity, the alliance was the most important factor for the AGP's defeat. However, the AGP and the BJP would not have done better if they had stayed apart.

> The Congress (I)'s victory in Assam was indeed expected this time. The ruling AGP that came to power in the state for the second time after a gap of five years in 1996 has failed to deliver. And after the BJP clinched a poll eve alliance with Mr. Mahanta and his 'boys' the Congress (I) leaders in the state did not have to look back at all. The anger against the AGP was indeed there and if proof was needed, it came in the crushing defeat suffered by Mahanta himself in one of the two constituencies he contested this time. In this sense, the change in Assam is indeed a reflection of the anger the voters had against the AGP: a reversal of the 1996 verdict when the Congress (I) lost to the AGP. (*The Hindu*, 21 May 2001)

REGION-WISE ANALYSIS

The voting pattern in constituencies dominated by communities like immigrant Muslims, tea-tribes, and STs reflect an interesting trend The AGP–BJP alliance failed to neutralize the apprehension and suspicion of religious minorities about the BJP's political ideology and agenda. The decision to go in for alliance with BJP had cost the AGP a significant number of Muslim votes. The CSDS survey shows that the Congress got an overwhelming 57 per cent of votes among the Muslims. The AGP–BJP counter-mobilization also worked in 10 constituencies. The election results of Hojai, Gauripur and Dhubri clearly prove this fact. Votes of the tea-garden workers and their families have traditionally sided with Congress. In the 2001 elections, the Congress secured 10 percentage points more than its state average (49.1) but won 19 out of 28 seats. The AGP and BJP alliance, on the other hand, could retain eight seats with 35.8 per cent of votes and BJP could manage to increase its support base among tea communities.

In the tribal belt, the massive turnout of voters close to 80 percent indicates the prevailing assertive behaviour of the tribal electorate in support of their ethnic identity. The Congress did not get the major chunk of ST votes, but it did bolster itself in non-Bodo areas to pick up 8 seats with 30.3 per cent of votes—a big gain compared to the

1991 and 1996 assembly elections when it could win only one seat. The Bodo belt area voted entirely for the ABSU–BPAC candidates. An analysis of the voting pattern by other social variables indicates a continuity of the pattern noticed in the previous elections. The victory of Congress was indeed expected in this election.

MIXED VERDICT:
2004 LOK SABHA ELECTIONS

The anti-incumbency wave that swept across the country did not have a distinct impact on the electorate in the state. The Congress government in the state was three years old, yet there were no sign of the usual anti-incumbency mood. Absence of anti-incumbency does not, however, mean the vote was in favour of the ruling Congress party. The state witnessed a triangular contest among the Congress, the BJP and the AGP. The Congress fought the election alone in the absence of any viable partner unlike in the rest of the country. It won nine seats though the vote share dropped to 35 per cent. The AGP won two seats, an improvement upon its disastrous show in the previous parliamentary and assembly elections. The BJP also won two seats. The BJP however, tied up with the Janata Dal(U) in Kaliabor constituency and supported the ABSU-led independent candidate in Kokrajhar constituency, which is mostly dominated by Bodos. The most significant aspect of this election is that the traditional Congress supporters such as the tea garden communities did not fully repose their faith on the Congress party. This was apparent from the defeat of Pradesh Congress Committee president Mr Paban Singh Ghatowar in Dibrugarh constituency where the tea garden communities hold the key. The Congress party had never lost this constituency since the first Lok Sabha election held in 1952. On the other hand, the Congress won the Autonomous District constituency where dominant tribal groups, namely the Karbis, have tended to favour the ASDC candidate Jayanta Rangpi who later joined with CPI(ML). But probably the most spectacular victory for the Congress was its success in defeating BJP candidate Bhupen Hazarika, a popular icon in the state. The political competition among the parties in this election was so intense that the chief minister himself confessed during a press conference that managing to win seats this time was not an easy task as the winning margin between the winners and losers was very narrow.

The BJP failed to make any significant breakthrough in terms of seat as its organizational base was relatively weak, and the party was relatively devoid of capable leaders. The regional party AGP managed to regain its recognition at national level by winning two seats after its debacle in the 1998 and 1999 elections, when it won no seats. The results thus reflect the signs of resurgence to a certain extent of regionalism in the state. The revival of the AGP may be credited to the change in leadership and the return of dissident leaders to its fold. The Left Democratic Alliance, however, failed to win any seat although its vote share showed a marked increase. An independent candidate backed by the ABSU and supported by BJP could retain the Bodo-dominant Kokrajhar constituency with the highest margin of votes in the state. The AGP too did not field any candidate in this constituency. On the whole, the mandate was a mixed one signalling diverse electoral choices.

ISSUES THAT MATTERED

No single issue had emerged as the central issue in this election. Interestingly, in the absence of a general wave in favour of any political party in the state, most of the parties seem to have played their old tunes to woo the voters. The ruling BJP at the Centre, which embarked on the 'India Shining' plank to attract voters in most parts of the country, has laid emphasis in Assam mainly on the perennial influx issue and repeal of IMDT Act. Undoubtedly, this is a serious political issue and the central and state governments should have taken corrective measures long back when the Assam Movement was launched for detection and extradition of foreign nationals from Assam. But electoral politics became so intricately related to this issue that it itself took the form of an incurable endemic disorder that had become a necessity for sustainability of vote-bank politics of its ruling clique. The regional formation of AGP, a party which was voted to power for two terms by the people in the state with the hope that their identity crisis would be taken care of by taking appropriate steps, got trapped in the same political mould like that of its predecessors as the politics to retain power prevailed over it. Naturally politics grew in the state centring on this issue. The Congress and the BJP who are arch-rivals in power politics have been politicking on it by taking diametrically opposite stand of protecting the interests and rights of the religious minority. The pertinent point of resolving the issue in conformity with the Assam Accord was totally ignored. The Congress has always been opposing the demand for scrapping the Act as its poll plank in the minority-dominated areas. The people belonging to the minority community, particularly in the border areas, hence, always remain apprehensive of their status in the country.

Interestingly, when the question regarding opinion on the issue of IMDT Act was asked during the 2004 post-poll survey conducted by CSDS, 21.2 per cent felt that the Act should be repealed, 10.4 per cent said it should continue, while 14.1 per cent commented that it should be strengthened and 54 per cent seemed to be ignorant about the problem. The Muslim population by and large plays a decisive role in the Assam elections. They have become more and more relevant in electoral terms because of their increasing numbers.

The Congress has enjoyed the unflinching support of these communities since Independence except during the 1985 and 1996 elections, when a split in the Muslim vote was inevitable due to the emergence of the significance held by regional, ethnic and cultural based parties in Assam politics. Therefore, terms such as division and polarization with regard to Muslim votes have a special relevance in the context of Assam politics even at the threshold of the 21st century. The Congress party by opposing the repeal of the IMDT Act as well as by assuring permanent land pattas and other backward status to char dwellers in Assam has undoubtedly endeared itself to these people, who happen to constitute their traditional vote bank.

WHO VOTED FOR WHOM

The Congress support base among the minorities remained intact as indicated by the party's victory in Muslim-dominated seats. It was

Table 5.5 *Who Voted for Whom: 2004 Lok Sabha Elections*

Community	INC	BJP	AGP
Upper Castes	33	33	20
OBCs	26	31	28
Adivasis	24	29	10
Muslims	66	8	14

Source: National election post poll survey, CSDS 2004. Sample size 1549.
Note: All figures are in percentage based on Assam sample of the post-poll survey.

apparent from the election survey (Table 5.5) that the religious minorities rallied on the side of the Congress and the immigrant linguistic Hindu minorities supported the BJP, while the indigenous people seem to have supported the AGP. Hindu polarization in Assam invariably consolidates the Muslim votes in a more organized way. It appears that the voter turnout in these areas was significantly high and it was a clear indication that the Congress regained Muslim support in this election. The state-wide post-poll survey undertaken by the CSDS with a sample size of 1,549 confirms this reading. The survey data show that the Congress got an overwhelming 66 per cent of votes among the Muslim respondents, compared to only 14 per cent for the AGP and a negligible 8 per cent for the BJP. The tea labourers in Assam have always played a significant role in the electoral politics. They belong mostly to Adivasi[2] tribe communities. The results of almost 30 assembly constituencies in Assam are largely determined by votes of these communities. These communities, traditionally considered as 'vote bank' for Congress, had always played a decisive role in the

[2] Adivasis in Assam are also known as 'tea community' or 'tea-tribe community'. It is a composite group that consists of those whose ancestors migrated as tea-garden workers from Central and Eastern India during the period of British rule. For a long time, these migrant workers did not have much interaction with the world outside the plantations, as they were deliberately kept insulated within tea garden premises by the plantation management. Due to the absence of communication facilities in the early years, the workers gradually lost contact with their native places, thus becoming permanent residents of the state. Presently, the Adivasis are included in the OBC category and have been raising demand for being recognized as an ST group in the state.

repeated victory of Congress candidates from Upper Assam. But in this election these workers did not extend their support in any way they did earlier to the party. This was evident in the performance of Congress candidates in areas dominated by tea-garden communities. On the other hand, the AGP pulled off a surprise when its candidate, a former president of AASU, Sarbananda Sonowal, won the seat by defeating the BJP youth leader candidate and former general secretary of All Assam Tea Tribes Students' Association (ATTSA), Kamakhaya Prasad Tasha, who managed to take away a huge chunk of the tea garden votes from the Congress. Further, the low victory margin of Bijoy Krishna Handique in Jorhat constituency, the defeat of the Congress candidate in the by-election to the Mariani constituency and decline of the party's vote share in tea-dominant assembly segments represented by ministers clearly reveal the erosion of its support base among these communities (Table 5.5). INTUC, the oldest labour organization having allegiance to the Congress, had been playing an important role through its affiliate, the Assam Chah Mazdoor Sangha, in order to consolidate its political hold on the tea-garden workers since 1947. The situation, however, seemed to have changed drastically in later years. The AGP too realized the impact of INTUC's reach and its ability to transform its trade union support into votes for the Congress. Therefore, AGP and BJP too have also started their own pockets of influence in the tea belt. However, it was seen that hardly any endeavour was made by the INTUC unions of the tea-garden workers to improve their socio-economic condition. Even the state government never did exert any pressure on the management to ensure justice to the plantation workers. Although the labour conference on the wage policy during the Second Five-Year Plan envisaged a specific guideline for calculation of minimum wage of a worker, the government of Assam did not even direct the tea management to follow this law for the tea plantation workers. Consequently, the tea management followed a peculiar policy in this context. Hence non-fulfilment of their demands like land settlement of small tea growers, non-payment of full bonus and wages fixed by the state government might have attributed to the decline of Congress's support base among the tea garden communities.

Social Background and Party Preferences

The National Election Study (NES) indicates a change in the pattern of voting noticed in this election as compared to the previous election. The Congress had a higher share of votes among the Muslim voters in this election, who constitute nearly 28 per cent of the total electorate. The BJP seems to have done well among all other communities except among Muslims. It is the BJP that leads the Congress among the Hindu upper castes. But then this is not much of a surprise since the Hindu upper castes have long been alienated from the Congress. The BJP has been poaching on the traditional social base of the AGP by converting Assamese nationalism into Hindu nationalism. Among the OBC communities, the BJP led while the Congress and AGP were almost evenly matched. The Congress is popular among the economically backward voters. Even among the lower middle class voters the Congress had the lead over the BJP and AGP. While the BJP and AGP did well among the well-to-do sections of society, in both respects the Congress got nearly twice as many votes from the worst-off than it got from the well-off. The BJP has the same class profile as it has in the rest of the country: the richer and more educated the people, the higher the vote for BJP. The Congress had a clear lead among voters from all age-groups and it appears that the Congress performed better among old age voters. Locality-wise voting pattern indicates that the Congress performed better than BJP and AGP among the rural voters. The BJP, on the other hand, did very well among the urban voters, while the support for AGP among urban and rural voters was almost equal. The 2004 verdict in the state presents a mixed scenario. While the election was largely a victory for the Congress, it was no less a boost for the sagging morale of the regional party.

ALL INDIA UNITED DEMOCRATIC FRONT

The All India United Democratic Front (AIUDF)[3] emerged in 2005 as a major force to reckon with in Assam politics. With its emergence, 'minority politics' opened up some new dimensions in the

---

[3] On 2 February 2009, the leader of the Assam United Democratic Forum (AUDF), Badruddin Ajmal, relaunched the party in other states of India through a press meet in New Delhi and renamed it as AIUDF.

political discourse of Assam. The party emerged after the Supreme Court verdict on the IMDT Act being unconstitutional. In 1983, the Indian parliament had passed the IMDT Act, a legislation on immigration applicable to the state of Assam. Since then, the politics of Assam is being dominated by this IMDT Act as elections have been fought with parties supporting either side of the IMDT divide. The Congress and Left parties supported the Act, while the BJP and AGP opposed it. After the Supreme Court's verdict, following a petition filed by Sarbananda Sonowal, in an effort to retain the vote bank of the Muslims, the Congress passed an ordinance that was almost the same as the IM(DT). Despite this, many minority organizations blamed Chief Minister Tarun Gogoi for not taking firm stand to retain the Act. Mr Badruddin Ajmal, the state unit president of Jamiat Ulema-e-Hind, tried to unite the minority-based organizations of the state so as to build public opinion against the repeal of the IM(DT) Act and the Congress government's stand on the IMDT issue. Amidst this state of affairs, a new political party, AUDF, came into existence.

Muslims, who had been traditionally favouring the Congress party, slowly realized that the party had not lived up to their expectations. The resultant simmering discontent among the Muslim community in Assam was tapped by the AIUDF, whose birth was a consequence of the political dynamics in the state and which has captured the attention of political analysts following the electoral successes it achieved in the state. Although there are a lot of differences in the political economy of UP and Assam, one thing which is common to both and which could be of interest to students of state politics is the almost simultaneous emergence of new Muslim political outfits in these two states in the last few years. The kind of enthusiasm of these formations generated among the Muslims in these states is really interesting to note, yet in the electoral arena the new political organizations have not been uniformly successful in their performance.

BEGINNING OF A COALITION ERA:
2006 ASSEMBLY ELECTION

The assembly elections of 2006 was the most fragmented one, ushering in an era of coalition politics in the state. This marked a major shift in the state politics. The Congress party showed resilience and an ability to form useful alliance as this election has brought to an end the winning of a single party by majority for the first time in the electoral history of Assam. With this election, the process of political fragmentation that begun in the state since the 1985 elections appears to have reached its culmination (Yadav and Kumar 2006). The results reflected reflect the deep-rooted fractured politics of the state with every community asserting its position. The state witnessed a clear fragmentation along ethnic lines, with AGP managing to retain its ethnic Assamese votes and BJP strengthening its hold among the Bengali Hindus and the Bodo communities, while the Bengali-speaking immigrant Muslims supported the newly formed AUDF. Thus, the state politics has moved from an era of catch all formations to that of cleavage-based politics in extreme form.

The Congress party emerged as the single largest party by winning 53 seats with 31.08 per cent votes. With the end of era of one-party rule in the state, the Congress could reach the magic figure of 64 in the 126-member assembly with the help of 12 MLAs of BPPF led by Hagrama Mahilary, a former militant, who signed the Bodo Accord in 2003. It is for the first time in the history of post-Independence Assam that the indigenous Bodo community played such a prominent role in the formation of government.

The AGP secured 24 seats with 20.39 per cent of votes. In terms of seats and votes, it gained four seats and marginally improved in terms of percentage of votes than the last assembly elections. Despite several opportunities offered by the party in power, it appeared that the AGP had failed to take advantage of the situation. The scrapping of the controversial IM(DT) Act was seen by many as a new problem before the Congress. But the AGP had been in considerable disarray and wrecked by splits, which made it unable to capitalize on this issue. Besides, this election did not carry any wave, either pro-establishment or in favour of any particular party. Even the exit poll and post-poll survey conducted by CSDS found that only 41 per cent of the respondents were in favour of giving the incumbent government another chance, while 55 per cent were opposed to its continuation. The survey found a moderate level of satisfaction with the government and the incumbent CM but strong anxiety about levels of corruption and on the crucial question of immigration issue. For fear of losing Muslim votes, the AGP kept distance from BJP in this election. The AGP contested the poll under seat sharing agreement with CPI, CPM, ASDC, SP, Trinamul Gana Parishad and the Rabiram faction of BPPF. The multipolar nature of political competition thus emerged with greater clarity than before in this election. The state has experienced a clear fragmentation of votes along ethnic lines. In fact, with this election the process of political and ethnic fragmentation that had begun with the Assam Movement reached its logical culmination.

The Congress party was considerably weakened and forced into a coalition to hold on to power. In more ways than one, this was a verdict against the ruling Congress. Perhaps what saved it was that the previous AGP government had received an even more negative rating in most opinion polls. Despite several opportunities offered by the party in power, it seems that the AGP failed to take advantage of the situation. In considerable disarray and wracked by splits (Prafulla Mahanta, the former chief minister, left the party with his breakaway faction: the AGP (Progressive)) the party was unable to capitalize on the poor record of the Congress government.

The split in the AGP led to a major breakup in its traditional vote bank, which undoubtedly benefitted both the Congress and the BJP. Even the exit poll and post poll survey data (CSDS 2006) found that only 41 per cent of the respondents were in favour of giving the incumbent government another chance, while 55 per cent were opposed to its continuation. The survey did indicate a moderate level of satisfaction with the government and the incumbent CM, but strong anxiety about the high levels of corruption and on the crucial question of immigration. On the whole, the mandate was against the AGP-led alliance, clearly indicative of its declining support base among the Muslim, SC and ST communities.

CHALLENGES TO CONGRESS

The Supreme Court judgment (12 July 2005) on IMDT Act, 1983 as unconstitutional just before the election came as a blow to minorities who blamed the Congress for not defending the Act strongly. The court judgment had actually polarized Assam. The Congress tried to allay their fears proclaiming the Foreigners (Tribunals for Assam) order of 2006. But this too has failed to satisfy the leaders of the minority communities. Consequently to protect their interests they left the Congress and formed this new party. The formation of the AUDF, a conglomerate of twenty religious and linguistic minorities on the eve of elections demonstrated the political clout wielded by its opponents. It posed a challenge to the Congress base among religious minorities, especially in the immigrant settlers in the char areas. The trajectory of change in Assam has been towards AIUDF which appears to have weaned away Muslim supporters of Congress. The party has weakened and forced into a coalition with just about manage to hold on to power. As between the 2001 assembly elections and 2006 assembly elections, the ruling party lost nearly 9 per cent votes and 17 seats. In any other state a negative swing of 9 points and a vote share of just 31 per cent would have spelt a sure electoral disaster for the party (Yadav and Kumar 2006). The post-poll and exit poll survey conducted by the CSDS (Table 5.13) clearly reveals that as many as 36 per cent of Assamese-speaking Muslims and 38 per cent of Bengali-speaking Muslims voted for the Congress. But this is poor consolation for a party that enjoyed the support of 52 and 72 per cent of these two groups, respectively, in the 2004 Lok Sabha elections when the AIUDF had not emerged. Thus, this election marks a major shift in the politics of the state.

A FRACTURED VERDICT: 2009 LOK SABHA

The verdict in Assam has far-reaching implications for the state's politics. Against extensive fears of a wipe out, the Congress party got away with a minor loss of two seats from its tally of nine in the 2004, and a minor loss of just one percentage point of votes. The AIUDF, which contested the Lok Sabha election for the first time, polled 16.1 per cent of votes and won one seat (Table 5.6). The BJP and its alliance partner, the AGP polled 30.8 per cent of vote. The alliance was expected to sweep Assam by consolidating the Hindu votes because the AIUDF was projected to deprive the Congress of its Muslim votes.

Table 5.6 *Lok Sabha Results: Changeover from 2004 to 2009 in Assam*

Party	Seat Contested 2009	Seats Won 2009	Seat Change from 2004	Vote (%) 2009	Vote Change from 2004
INC	13	7	−2	34.89	−0.18
BJP	7	4	2	16.21	−6.73
AGP	6	1	−1	14.60	−5.35
AUDF	9	1	1	16.10	16.10
BPPF	2	1	1	5.41	5.41
Others	121	0	0	12.79	−9.24

Source: CSDS Data Unit.

However, it worked differently. Actually the Congress has managed to guard its fortress among Assamese speaking Muslims. The alliance between AGP and the BJP hit both the parties. Association with BJP cost AGP its Muslim votes while association with AGP cost the BJP its Bengali-speaking Hindu votes. Congress was the beneficiary since it gained among Bengali-speaking Hindus in addition to strengthening its Muslim vote (*The Hindu*, 26 May 2009). Thus, the AGP–BJP alliance seems to have paid the price for AGP's pro-Assamese regional sentiment and BJP's Hindutva ideology in the form of Bengali-speaking Hindu votes and Assamese-speaking Muslim votes.

REGION-WISE ANALYSIS

The Congress victory in the 2009 Lok Sabha elections was essentially the by-product of a sweep in select regions.[4] In Upper Assam, dominated by tea garden areas, the Congress vote base among the

---

[4] To understand society and politics in Assam, the state may be divided into three regions: Upper Assam or tea areas, Barak Valley and Lower Assam. Tea belt area includes Dibrugarh, Jorhat, and Tezpur and Lakhimpur constituencies; Barak Valley is named after Barak River, situated in the southern part of Assam. It consists of three districts, namely Cachar, Karimgang and Hailakandi. Majority of the people speak a dialect of Bengali, which is known as Sylheti and Lower Assam is comprised of the districts of Kamrup, Darrang and Nagaon.

tea community[5] was relatively intact in the two key constituencies, namely Dibrugarh and Jorhat. INTUC's allegiance to the Congress has helped retain Congress votes in this region. The BJP, however, made inroads into the tea-garden dominated areas, which were traditionally considered a Congress bastion (Table 5.7).

The Muslims in Assam mainly concentrate in the lower districts of the Brahmaputra Valley and Barak Valley districts. The six valley districts of Assam have more than 50 per cent Muslims in their total population. The voting pattern of the Muslim-dominated constituencies, therefore, had become crucial in this election. Our survey data shows[6] that the Congress lost virtually all its immigrant Muslim voters with 78 per cent of them voting for the AIUDF. But among the Assamese Muslims, the Congress secured 75 per cent support, a gain of 23 per cent over 2004 among Muslims of this region. The AGP–BJP combine lost 13 percentage points among Assamese Muslims. The alliance with the BJP cost the AGP a significant number of Muslim votes (Table 5.8). This time, the alliance could manage only about 35 per cent of the vote. The beneficiary of this failure was the Congress, which gained 21 per cent points among Bengali-speaking Hindus. The alliance seems to have paid the price for the AGP's anti-Bengali stance and the BJP's anti-Muslim stance in the form of Bengali-speaking Hindu votes and the Assamese-speaking Muslim votes.

---

[5] What is known as the 'tea community' or 'tea-tribe community' in Assam today is a composite group that consists of those whose ancestors migrated as tea-garden workers from Central and East India during the period of British rule and thereafter. For a long time, these migrant workers could not have much interaction with the world outside the plantations, as they were deliberately kept insulated by the plantation management.

[6] A cross-section sample survey was conducted in Assam as part of the NES 2009. This study was independently supported by UGC—UGC major research project, 'A Study of the 15th General Elections to Lok Sabha in the State Assam' (F. No 5-21/2008/HRP). The study included post-poll survey carried out for the 2009 Lok Sabha elections and the 2011 assembly elections in collaboration with the Lokniti programme of the CSDS. The sample size for the 2009 Lok Sabha elections was 1,402, while that for the 2011 Assam Assembly elections was 3,347.

Table 5.7 *Region-wise Voting Pattern in Assam, 2009*

Regions	Total Seats	Turnout Seats %	Congress		BJP		AGP		BPPF		AUDF		ASDC		Others	
			Won	Vote	Won	Vote	Won	Vote	Won	Vote	Won	Vote	Won	Vote	Won	Vote
Barak Valley	3	67.7	2	35.3	1	26.6	0	0.0	0	0.0	0	24.5	0	6.6	0	7.0
Lower Assam	5	71.0	1	28.0	2	15.9	0	10.0	1	13.0	1	20.0	0	0	0	13.2
Upper Assam	6	68.8	4	41.4	1	12.8	1	24.2	0	0.0	0	9.4	0	0	0	12.1
Total	14	69.5	7	34.9	4	16.2	1	14.6	1	5.4	1	16.1	0	1.0	0	12.8

Source: CSDS Data Unit, 2009.

Table 5.8 *Muslim Votes in 2009 Compared to 2004*

Party	2009	Swing from 2004
Congress	32	−31
AGP–BJP	5	−19
AIUDF	60	+60
Others	3	−10

Source: CSDS Data Unit.
Note: Vote shares for 2009 are in per cent, while swings are in percentage points. AIUDF did not exist in 2004. In the last elections, the AGP and the BJP contested separately. The swings are calculated by merging the individual vote share for the two parties for 2004; $N = 1,402$.

CONGRESS IN SURVIVAL MODE: 2011 ASSEMBLY ELECTIONS

The 2011 assembly elections marked the beginning of a new phase in the state politics. Belying all speculations and expectations of a fragmented verdict, the mandate has been clear and decisive in the 2011 assembly elections. The state has switched back to one-party rule from a coalition era. The Congress secured this unambiguous verdict in spite of the allegations of corruption by the Opposition parties, sections of the media and civil society. Meanwhile, the main Opposition party, the AGP, suffered a humiliation at the hustings as did the BJP, with several of their bigwigs, including both party chiefs, biting the dusts. The AIUDF and Bodoland People's Front (BPF) have improved their tally and the Trinamool Congress has managed to open its account by winning one seat. But the big puzzle is: how did the Congress manage to get such a massive victory? Was the troubled state really destined to be on the road to recovery?

What worked in the in the favour of Congress was its focus on the questions of peace, development and identity. There seemed a real possibility of a political solution to the vexed problem of militancy in the state. By engaging with dominant militant groups across the negotiation table and initiating a much-awaited peace process without any preconditions on the issue of sovereignty after 30 long years, the Gogoi government won the confidence of the state's peace-loving people, who have greatly suffered from the violence and insecurity generated by insurgent activities. The emergence of the AIUDF did cost the Congress a portion of immigrant Muslim votes, but the Congress regained its lost strength reasonably well by wooing Assamese-speaking Muslims and some Assamese-speaking Hindus who had earlier allied with the AGP and BJP, respectively. Thus the gains of the Congress were across all sections by making it a catch-all party. What was more surprising is that AIUDF could become the main Opposition party in this election by surpassing AGP and other national parties. The results reiterate the fact that to win in a state, what is most important is to empower state leaders instead of depending on national leaders. With the win for three consecutive terms, Tarun Gogoi joined the illustrious list of 'empowered chief ministers'. The lesson is that the regional is indeed the new national. The Congress win for third term is a rare achievement in an age when anti-incumbency is a part of the political lexicon.

THE VERDICT

With an impressive 76.03 per cent turnout of votes, this election was significant for a variety of reasons. The insurgency outfit, ULFA, did not call for a poll boycott, and there was no major disruption in the democratic process. Pre-poll alliance was not there in this election, except the seat adjustment among a few parties. The Congress and the BJP fought the elections each on their own. The Congress party could win absolute majority with 78 seats and 39.38 per cent of votes (Table 5.2), thereby reversing the trend before 1986 assembly elections. On the contrary, the main Opposition, AGP, suffered a big humiliation. The party which was in power for two terms fell short of even to qualify as the main Opposition party. In spite of several mergers, the AGP was still divided into three camps, separately associated with Prafulla Mahanta, Chandra Mohan Patowary and Brindabon Goswami. Besides, AGP's seat adjustments at the local level with BPPF led by Ganashakti Party and ASDC did not improve its tally, as these parties are influential only in small pockets. Although the AGP had not forged any alliance with BJP in the election, it also did not put up any candidate against the BJP party president in the constituency, and this raised fundamental questions about the aims and objectives of a

Table 5.9 *Region-wise Analysis of Results: Assembly Elections, 2011*

Regions	Total Seats	Turnout	Congress Won	Congress Vote (%)	AGP Won	AGP Vote (%)	BJP Won	BJP Vote (%)	AIUDF Won	AIUDF Vote (%)	BPPF Won	BPPF Vote (%)	Other Won	Other Vote (%)
Barak Valley	20	70.9	18	47.8	1	4.8	0	17.4	1	11.4	0	0.0	0	18.7
Lower Assam	50	78.8	16	30.4	3	15.9	3	8.4	13	17.1	12	13.6	3	14.6
Upper Assam	56	75.0	44	45.5	6	20.6	2	12.6	4	8.4	0	0.7	0	12.2
Total	126	75.9	78	39.4	10	16.3	5	11.5	18	12.6	12	6.1	3	14.2

Source: CSDS Data Unit, 2011.

regional party. Religious minorities and secular segments considered such stand as an antithesis of the regional plank of the AGP. The BJP too had its seats and vote share reduced compared to the last assembly elections. The Left parties, like in the previous election, failed to open an account (Table 5.9).

EXPLAINING CONGRESS'S VICTORY

The Congress started with an advantage in both parliamentary and assembly elections. More importantly, in its choice of candidates and in its strategy of entering into coalitions, the Congress was more circumspect and successful. The Congress party presented a blend of new and old faces that worked well compared to the main Opposition party, AGP. Moreover, the Congress party could recover its old role of a grand unifier of divergent social and economic forces. The party's decision not to form alliance with AIUDF also paid dividends. When asked during the assembly post-poll survey whether voters wanted the Congress to have an alliance with the AIUDF, 43 per cent Congress supporters answered in the negative. This endorses the stand taken by the party. As already discussed, the emergence of the AIUDF did cost the Congress a portion of immigrant Muslim votes, but the Congress could regain its lost strength reasonably well by wooing the Assamese-speaking Muslims and part of the Assamese-speaking Hindus having allegiance mainly to the AGP and BJP. Thus the gains of the Congress across all sections made it more of a 'catch-all' party in Assam. However, the Congress faced the challenge of retaining its Muslim support in the state where the AIUDF took away a large chunk of the Muslim vote.

But electoral strategies help only when the ruling party has manifested some ability to deliver. On this count, the Congress in Assam fared well. Peace initiatives and popular schemes of the central government appear to have contributed greatly to the Congress victory. The emphasis on peace talks with the insurgent groups and development of the state, instead of playing into the hands of sectional interests, paid rich dividends to the Congress. People who have lived under the shadow of the gun can understand how valuable peace is. Assam has been reeling from violence and insecurity for nearly a quarter of a century. The initiation of peace dialogue with the ULFA proved to be the Congress's trump card. When asked during the post-election survey whether Congress government has succeeded in solving insurgency problem during last five years almost 53 per cent opined in the affirmative.

Pro-poor initiatives of the government such as the National Rural Employment Guarantee Scheme (NREGS) and the farm loan waiver scheme may not have fully exerted their impact on the people, but they did create a positive climate for the incumbent party, even though weak delivery systems have prevented the benefits from reaching the targeted populations. The NREGS was extremely popular across the state. Besides, a review of the welfare measures introduced by the incumbent government makes it clear why the Congress could get such a mandate. As many as 58 lakh schoolchildren have been getting mid-day meals, which means that at least 40 lakh families benefited. Over 92,000 students were given free computers and laptops on getting first division marks in the high school finals. About 1.35 lakh girl students of classes IX and X in rural areas were given a bicycle each. Over 1.5 lakh teachers and employees of non-government schools (who earn modest salaries) were given monthly support ranging from ₹2,000 to ₹3,500. Headmasters of 16,300 'venture' schools were given additional financial support. Besides, jobs of 7,000 teachers appointed during the AGP regime under Operation Blackboard were regularized (Talukdar 2011).

GOVERNANCE RECORD

In this backdrop, the survey data show that reasonable proportion of the population was at least partially (somewhat) satisfied with the performance of the government (Table 5.10). It is noteworthy that this satisfaction remained constant and in fact slightly increased over a period of five years, which in itself is an achievement. As mentioned above, the introduction of several new social welfare schemes to benefit the students, girl child, women and unemployed, and cash assistance to farmers, microfinance to self-help groups to engage rural women in employment-generation activities have ensured this satisfaction

Table 5.10 *Level of Satisfaction with the State Government*

Satisfaction with Congress Government in the State	Year		
	2006	2009	2011
Fully Satisfied	15	16	15
Somewhat Satisfied	43	49	48
Somewhat Dissatisfied	16	17	15
Fully Dissatisfied	23	11	10
No Opinion	3	7	11

Source: CSDS Data Unit.

Note: Sample size in 2006 was 2,702; 1,402 in 2009; and 3,348 in 2011.

Table 5.11 *Assessment of the State Government on Major Issues*

Areas	2006 Improved/	Deteriorated	2011 Improved/	Deteriorated
Condition of roads	65	29	74	24
Supply of electricity	48	39	65	32
Supply of drinking water	41	43	49	45
Quality of education in government schools	49	36	59	34
Medical facilities in government hospitals	37	48	73	22
Law and order situation	44	29	58	23

Source: Assam Assembly post-poll surveys, 2006 and 2011.

level. As per the survey data, voters believed that many services and facilities as also the infrastructure in the state improved between 2004 and 2009. This includes perception of improvement regarding roads, electricity, drinking water, education, health facilities and law and order (Table 5.11).

Given this assessment of performance of the government, it is not surprising that the then chief minister, Tarun Gogoi, would be a popular leader in the state with a capacity to fetch votes and win the election. What is more important is the long-term popularity of

Table 5.12 *Popularity of Chief Minister: 2001–2011*

	2001	2004	2006	2009	2011
Tarun Gogoi	20	37	33	38	38
Prafulla Mahanta	20	4	2	4	8

Source: CSDS Data Unit. Sample size in 2001 was 1,236; in 2004 was 1,549; in 2006 was 2,702; in 2009 was 1,402; and in 2011 was 3,348.

Notes: 1. Responses above are to an open-ended question. 2. Question asked in the surveys, 'After this election, who would you prefer as the next chief minister of Assam?' (no names were offered to those being interviewed; all responses are spontaneous and were post-coded). 3. NC: names Not Coded in those years as the responses were insignificant; NA: Not Applicable. 4. Other important names mentioned by respondents for 2011 were Himanta Biswa Sarma (6%) and Badrudin Ajmal (8%).

Gogoi. We have survey data for a full decade and at the starting point in 2001, both Gogoi of Congress and Prafulla Kumar Mahanta of AGP had the same popularity rating of 20 per cent each. Table 5.12 reports the trend which shows how Gogoi has almost doubled his popularity while Mahanta has lost the same.

POPULARITY OF CHIEF MINISTER

The revival of the Congress was not caused by overcoming of the endemic organizational weakness that it had suffered from. It took place without any organizational revival. Besides, the party could not increase its traditional bases. In the first term of his office, Tarun Gogoi appeared capable of delivering. He stabilized the financial side of the state economy, and salaries were made regular. The state also saw improvement in law and order to a great extent. This was more or less the general view of Tarun Gogoi's first term as the AGP-led government had left the state denuded and earned the reputation of not being able to pay even salary to the government employees.

The second term of Gogoi was marked by activities in the field of health with the work of two medical colleges being initiated—one at Jorhat and the other at Barpeta. However, the second term was replete with failures in many aspects. The most conspicuous of them all was the failure on the law and order front. Ethnic riots in Western Assam took many lives and made thousands homeless. Several camps became the only alternative for lakhs of people affected by the worst ever incident of bomb blast took place on 30 October 2008 in Guwahati and other parts of Assam, which shook not just the state but the psyche of the country as a whole. Along with the law and order situation, another malaise had started eating into the fabric of the government. Financial scams one after another were unleashed. The biggest among them being the ₹1,100 crore scam unleashed in the North Cachar Hills Autonomous Council. There was another area where the government failed measurably which was in handling the devastating floods that ravaged the state causing heavy loss to life and property in year 2010. The situation was handled with utmost casualness and lack of concern by the chief minister. However, despite all these lapses the Gogoi-led government came to power in a stronger way. This victory led to dissidence within a few of the party's members later. Gogoi did not want to part with the credit due to his junior colleagues whose dedicated effort brought about the landslide victory. Gogoi's agenda of promoting and projecting his son as a candidate in state politics came into the open. The result was open dissidence among party members, which continued for the whole term pushing aside governance to the back seat. All of the above cumulatively acted against his government in subsequent years.

SUPPORT BASE OF THE CONGRESS PARTY

In contemporary Assam, political fault lines are shaped at the cusp of community and language. Therefore, it may not be useful to inquire into political preferences of caste groups. Instead, we need to look at the choices made by the Hindu and Muslim communities—both of which are divided further into Bengali and Asomiya Hindus and Muslims. This is an outcome of the peculiar situation of the state and the agitation over the issue of outsiders/migrants. This means that the Asomiya identity shapes in the shadow of both language and community. As a result, political parties can either uphold only one identity and capitalize upon the support of that group or they can seek overlaps across communities and groups in search of a more broad-based and

Table 5.13 *Community-wise Support Base: 2006 and 2011*

	Congress		AIUDF		AGP		BJP	
Community	2006	2011	2006	2011	2006	2011	2006	2011
Assamese Muslims	39	55	32	16	13	11	4	4
Bengali Muslims	36	28	36	55	8	7	0	1
Assamese Hindus	25	34	3	0	31	34	10	8
Bengali Hindus	29	30	7	6	14	10	30	35
Others	38	41	2	5	23	11	13	8

Source: CSDS Data Unit.

Note: All figures in %; total number of respondents in 2006—Assamese Muslims (149), Bengali Muslims (398), Assamese Hindus (999), Bengali Hindus (336), Others (644); in 2011 total number of respondents—Assamese Muslims (205), Bengali Muslims (527), Assamese Hindus (977), Bengali Hindus (339), and Others (992).

electorally viable social alliance. The Congress's success over the one decade under review is based on the latter strategy and, conversely, the failure of AGP stems from its inability to become acceptable to different cross-sections of the Assamese society. As Table 5.13 shows, AIUDF has become a party of Bengali Muslims while BJP has become a party of Bengali Hindus. This polarization puts constraints on the two other parties—Congress and AGP. Congress's strategy to balance all social sections paid dividends in this situation.

The survey data reveals the vote share among Assamese Muslims increased from 39 per cent in 2006 to 55 per cent in 2011. However, it retained a major chunk of its vote among Bengali Muslims had reduced from 36 per cent to 28 per cent. Simultaneously, its vote share among Assamese Hindus went up to 34 per cent from 25 per cent in 2006 and among Bengali Hindus it increased to 30 per cent. This clearly reflects the ethnic Assamese voters are the key to the Congress success and party. It and also retained its base among Bengali Hindus. It is clear that going beyond religious threshold, the Congress carved out for itself the Assamese constituency and neutralized its opponents. The AIUDF did cost the Congress a portion of immigrant Muslim votes but regained its lost strength among the Assamese Muslims and

Bengali Hindus who had earlier voted for the AGP and BJP, respectively. Nevertheless, the polarization of Muslim votes has long-term implications for the state politics. Besides, the success of AIUDF and BPPF seemed to have encouraged the formation of smaller ethnic parties, causing even greater political fragmentation.

The advantage secured by the AGP, the main Opposition party, in power for two terms—to unite the people of the state to form a cohesive Assamese nationality—has failed over the years since its inception. A united AGP in this election after a period of painful separation of its incongruous faction, the AGP (Progressive), failed to capitalize on the failure of the Congress government to adequately address major issues concerning the state such as floods, erosion, impact of big dams, corruption, rapid population increase and so on. The AGP's sole mobilization plank in this election seemed to have evolved only around institutionalization of corruption. In reality, the issue of corruption did not probably touch the general public beyond a few urban locations. Besides, AGP's seat adjustments did not actually improve its tally as such parties have their influence only in small pockets. However, it is to be remembered that the structural reasons underlying the emergence of regional parties in Assam have not totally disappeared; rather these may be present in some areas even more intensely in their dormant state. The future of AGP in Assam lies not on short-term political alliances for occupying a few seats in elections, but on how it works for the dormant political desire of the hitherto unrepresented social forces under a larger federal political umbrella that can effectively strike a balance between the ruling segments and the minorities.

Of course, it was anticipated that the Congress party would come back for a third term, but the numbers were quite unexpected. Now the real question arises: how the Congress managed to win such a number and what prompted the people of Assam to oust the AGP? Instead of saying that it was a win for Congress this election may be termed as a failure of the irresponsible and divided Opposition. The main causes of the AGP's poll debacle in the 2011 Assam Assembly elections were the party's attitude towards its supporters in the grassroots level and an unwelcome atmosphere to enrol new generation leaders. In the process, the party which was formed after the six-year long Assam Agitation in 1985, giving a new ray of hope for Assamese society, has reached a vacuum in the present era of the state's politics. The fact that the party had only limited its base to the Brahmaputra Valley also contributed to the party's dismayed performance in the polls. Other than the said area, the party could not spread its support base. The party rather than asking for votes for forming the government should have asked for support of the people to form a strong Opposition in the state assembly. The AGP miserably failed to reach out to the masses by doing little as the Opposition party for two consecutive terms since 2001. Not only has this but the party's alliance to a separate ideology—that of the BJP—severely affected the party's vote share, as a result of which it lost a considerable number of assembly seats.

The AGP leadership should have morally accepted their responsibility for such a shaky election performance and not tarnished its own image by alleging some foul play on the part of the ruling party, such as tempering of electronic voting machines (EVMs), and accepted the verdict of the people gracefully. The Congress came back to power not because of the so-called development it brought to the state but because the Opposition helped the Congress to win by being weak and at the same time power-hungry.

Two key questions arise from the outcome. One is about the nature of party competition and the other is about the future of the social conflicts that have engulfed Assam for over three decades. On the surface, it may appear that for Assam the days of regional political forces are now over. The fact that AGP has failed to wrest power in last more than a decade might give strength to such an assessment. In the assembly elections of 2011, the AGP and the BJP struck a seat-sharing deal so as to avoid a split in their votes in the 2009 Lok Sabha elections. The alliance was expected to sweep Assam by consolidating the Hindu votes, but it did not bring the desired result. The electoral understanding failed to dispel the apprehensions of religious minorities about the BJP's political ideology and its agenda. Religious minorities and secular segments considered the alliance an antithesis of the regional plank of the AGP. This was the second time that the AGP faltered when fighting an election as a partner of BJP, the first time being in the 2001 assembly elections. The results clearly proved that pre-poll alliance between the AGP and the BJP helped the former to consolidate its position in the Brahmaputra Valley though at the cost of the party's regional character.

CONCLUSION

With the win for three consecutive terms, Tarun Gogoi has joined the illustrious list of 'empowered chief ministers'. The lesson is that the regional is indeed the new national. The Congress win for third term is a rare achievement in an age when anti-incumbency is a part of the political lexicon. The Congress Party's emphatic return to power in the state was the consequence of a perceived and deserved image of 'peace and development' during its rule in the state. It managed to retain power despite a pervasive image of corruption as the opposition was disunited and unable to raise issues of consequence to large sections of the electorate in the state. The Congress won due to a combination of factors, among which was promise of peace. The other promise that seems to have attracted voters to the Congress is development. This is not an ideological promise; this will come from good governance. If the Congress does not show evidence of real progress, the election victory in retrospect will only be seen as a victory due to the contingent political circumstance like a national position lacking confidence, a state-level opposition lacking promise, and new social force lacking unity and direction. State-level political forces in Assam arise mainly because of an inability of the political spectrum to accommodate hitherto unrepresented sections of the society in a symbolic manner. Underneath the apparent political supremacy of the Congress party, the state can still witness an unrest caused by more serious issues related to immigration of foreign nationals, rising prices and grievances of ethnic minorities and corruption, among others. The Congress party did not earn the victory; it was thrust on the party. Circumstantial factors, rather than any design and initiative that brought the Congress back to power is surely dependent on party's ability to sharpen its focus on addressing the structural issues of the state, if left unattended may snowball into major irritants.

This chapter has presented the causes for the recovery of Congress party with empirical and corollary evidence in the state for three decades in turn, in the next chapter, to discussing some important factors that may have a bearing for the changed political dynamics of the state.

REFERENCES

Asom Gana Parishad, 'Election Manifesto of Asom Gana Parishad. General Assembly Election', AGP Central Office Ambari, Guwahati, 2001.

Barua, Apurba, and Sandhya Goswami. 1999, 21 August–3 September. 'Fractured Identities and Politics in a Multi-ethnic State'. *Economic & Political Weekly* 34 (34–35): 2492–2501.

Dutta, Anubhab. 1998. 'Religious Influence in Assam Politics'. *The Assam Tribune*, 4 March.

Goswami, Manoranjan. 2009. 'A Wake Up Call for AGP'. *The Assam Tribune*, 23 May.

Goswami, Sandhya. 1998. 'Lok Sabha Election Results in Assam: An Analysis'. *The Assam Tribune*, 20 March.

———. 2003. 'Assam'. In *India's 1999 Elections and 20th Century Politics*, edited by Paul Wallace and Ramashray Roy. New Delhi: SAGE Publications.

———. 2003. 'Assam Multiple Realignments and Fragmentation of Party System'. *Journal of Indian School of Political Economy* 15 (1, 2 January): 220–247.

———. 2011a. 'Electoral Trends in Assam: Some Reflections'. *The Assam Tribune*, 19 March.

———. 2011b. 'The Congress's Assets in Assam'. *The Indian Express*, 17 May.

———. 2011c. 'Mandate for Peace in Assam'. *Economic & Political Weekly* 47 (23, 4–10 June): 20–22.

———. 2012. 'Changing Trends of Electoral Politics'. *Seminar* 640 (December). Available at: https://www.india-seminar.com/2012/640/640_sandhya_goswami.htm

———. 2014. 'Triumph for Congress in Assam'. In *Party Competition in Indian States*, edited by Suhas Palshikar, K. C. Suri, and Yogendra Yadav, 363–380. New Delhi: Oxford University Press.

Hussain, Wasbir. 2001. 'Elections under the Shadow of Gun'. *Economic & Political Weekly* 36 (5/6, 3–10 February): 442–444.

Misra, Udayon. 1989. 'Bodo Stir Complex Issues, Unattainable Demands'. *Economic & Political Weekly* 24 (21, 27 May): 1146–1149.

Srikanth, H. 2000. 'Militancy and Identity Politics in Assam'. *Economic & Political Weekly* 35 (47, 18 November).

Talukdar, Sushant. 2011. 'Assembly Elections 2011: Can Congress Do It a Third Time?' *The Hindu*, 3 April.

The Hindu, 'New Government in Assam (Editorial)', 21 May 2001.

The North East Times, 'AGP's Failures (Editorial)'. 30 March 2001.

Yadav, Yogendra. 2001. 'On Predictable Lines'. *Frontline*, 8 June.

———. 2008. 'The Paradox of Political Representation'. *Seminar* 586 (June). Available at: india-seminar.com/2008/586/586_yogendra_yadav.htm

Yadav, Yogendra, and Sanjay Kumar. 2006. 'Assembly Elections 2006: An Election Too Close to Call'. *The Hindu*, 9 April.

Shift towards Bharatiya Janata Party

The Bharatiya Janata Party's (BJP) victory in the Lok Sabha elections 2014 brought back a new version of single-party dominance in Indian politics. It is no doubt related to the creation of a coherent narrative of the nation, which the Opposition in its entirety has failed to build since 2014. The BJP and its allies have spent decades building a narrative of majoritarianism that has come to fruition now (Chandhoke 2014). The BJP's dominance originated in a strongly personalized leadership and it is also deeply entwined with an ideological insistence on Hindutva discourse, though meanings and emphases in the Hindutva discourse have kept shifting (Palshikar 2019). The resurgence of Hindu nationalism was a defining feature of Indian politics in the 1990s. Although the ideas and organization associated with the trend have roots in the early 20th century, yet they were politically marginalized for much of the post-Independence period. Even in the 1980s, the party was at periphery, capable of winning only two seats in the 1984 parliamentary elections. Yet by 1991, the BJP was the second-largest party in the country and by 1998 it was leading the ruling coalition. Perhaps more important, the ideology of Hindu nationalism or Hindutva (literally 'Hinduness') has become part of the ideological mainstream (Hibbard 2010, 115). The precipitous rise of Hindu nationalism in Indian politics can be explained in large measure by the changing attitude of the state leaders towards secular ideals of the Nehru period (Hasan 1990). The commitment to an inclusive social order, however, faded with Nehru's death in 1964, especially after the Emergency period. The Congress party thereafter sought to co-opt the rhetoric and symbols of Hindu nationalism for electoral consideration. Although majoritarian strategy worked for the Congress party in short term, most particularly in the party's 1984 electoral landslide, it had dire consequences later on. By overturning Nehruvian consensus, the Congress leaders helped to disembed the secular norms that had governed Indian public life for most of the post-Independence era (Hibbard 2010, 117). The communalization of the Indian politics under Congress rule in the 1980s perhaps helps to explain the dramatic and rapid nature of the BJP's rise in Indian politics. As religion is an essential part of the construction of collective identities and provides a sense of belonging to a larger community, this chapter examines how BJP's rise in the state became possible and why a particular ethnic identity has the propensity for mass appeal and politicization.

THE BJP'S RISE IN ASSAM

The ideology of Hindutva does not have much appeal in Assam as in the northern part of India for its uniquely different population composition, culture, history and belief systems. Moreover, the spread of Vaishnavism, particularly in the valley areas, contributed significantly towards the softening and, in many cases, obliteration of many inegalitarian social practices, rituals, orthodoxies and dogmas of Hindu caste system in the state. As a result, cultural organizations like the RSS, from the very beginning, adopted novel strategies customized to the complex particularities of this region in order to establish itself in the cultural and political imagination of the people. Moving away from its standard techniques of mobilizing support through the invocation of Hindu stereotypes like 'Ram' or 'Ayodhya', it instead has focused on adaptation of local cults and symbols such as those associated with Kamakhya and Sankardev, namely the Sattra tradition (Bhattacharjee 2016, 86–87). Further, the presence of a considerably large population of Muslims in the state, and the rising alarm of the natives to the accelerating influx of immigrants from Bangladesh, provided a tailor made ground for the RSS to operate in the region. Together these provided a congenial climate for the burgeoning of Hindutva in the region. Further, the proselytizing activities of the Christian missionaries among the tribals in the state since the colonial period gave the RSS an opportunity to play its anti-Christian card on the basis that Christianity has lured them to adopt a foreign culture and religion, thereby drawing them away from their traditional faiths. On these arguments, Hindutva seemed to have succeeded in gaining grounds in the tribal regions of Assam, through the social work of its affiliate, the Vanavasi Kalyan Ashram (VKA). It appears that the VKA has been increasingly active persuading tribals to eschew tribal religious practices in favour of Rama and Hanuman Puja by establishing a large network in the Adivasi areas. Though the RSS entered Assam as early as 1946, it could not create a significant impact in the beginning owing to its unpopularity fostered by the assassination of Mahatma Gandhi by a former RSS member in 1948 (Jaffrelot 2015). Thereafter, it concentrated mainly on strengthening its organization by creating networks through local notables, opening 'shakhas' (branches) and consolidating its activities. The 1950 earthquake in Assam provided the RSS one of its initial entry points to this region, when it undertook extensive relief work for the earthquake victims. The language agitation of 1959–1960 provided another opportunity to the RSS in the state, especially in building its support base among the Hindu Bengalis (Bhattacharjee 2016). Thereafter, in the late 1970s, the Assam Movement finally set the hard-wearing ground for the growth of Hindu nationalism. Pralay Kanungo remarked, 'Hindutva, in terms of strategy, shows admirable powers of adaptability-swinging from volatile and violent, to soft and silent—depending on the specificity of the context' (Kanungo 2011, 91).

THE REGIONAL CONTEXT

The spectre of illegal migration has long haunted the state of Assam and it remains one of the most contested issues in the politics of the state since the days of Partition. What is essentially a national issue has been allowed or encouraged to become an ethnic, linguistic and communal issue of the state by the governments ruling it at different time points. The Assam Movement against the foreign nationals issue thus provided a regional context with a broad 'national' appeal and it also befittingly fell within the framework of the BJP's ideological assertion of Hindu national identity. The BJP's rise in the 1990s was also marked by two distinct political developments: the decline of the Congress and the emergence of some new state-level parties (Chibber and Verma 2018). The emergence of regional and ethnic parties in the late 1980s in Assam has further contributed to BJP's rise. The BJP has flagged the importance of immigration issue in all its elections since the late 1980s as the the regional party AGP. This particular issue has become the most important issue for the RSS in the state. The insecurity aroused by the immigrants, particularly among the Assamese Hindus, has been subjugated largely by the RSS activists, who have time and again highlighted this problem as 'a threat to national security'. The RSS has used this sentiment to spread its tentacles in the state and build up its organization slowly. Although initially the Assamese Hindus from Brahmaputra Valley did not support BJP, yet the party's continued emphasis on illegal migration gradually changed the mindset among the middle class since the 1998 elections. The party began to resonate the demand of the AASU and AGP after coming to power at the Centre in 1998. Thereby, the party was able to make a dent in the Brahmaputra Valley for the first time in the 1999 Lok Sabha elections and gradually expand its support base (Table 6.1).

The BJP has not only succeeded in making its inroads in the Brahmaputra Valley but has also consolidated its position among the other indigenous communities. Apart from other factors, the BJP's rise could be attributed to its promise to repeal the IMDT Act, thereby allaying fears of the indigenous Assamese of being wiped out (Goswami 2012). The BJP slowly 'hijacked' the issue of illegal migration from the regional party AGP, which was born in 1985 as a

Table 6.1 *Performance of BJP in Assam Lok Sabha Elections: 1991–2019*

Year	Seat Secured	Votes Polled (%)
1991	2	09.60
1996	1	15.09
1998	1	24.47
1999	2	29.84
2004	2	22.94
2009	4	16.62
2019	10	36.05

Source: Election Commission of India.

result of the long-drawn Assam Movement for the expulsion of illegal foreign nationals from Assam. While other parties, both national and regional, have failed to address this issue concretely, the BJP took the opportunity to project itself as a party capable and credible enough to resolve this unaddressed issue. The BJP realized the fact that the state could be an ideal ground for its growth as it has a ready-made line of polarization between the Muslims of East Bengal origin on the one side and the Assamese-speaking Hindus on the other. Besides, the hill and plains tribal communities have also united on the illegal migrants issue. The Congress government, both at the Centre and in the state, showed apathy towards resolving the issues of deportation and detection of illegal foreigners. As a consequence, the focus of the party has shifted towards the issue of Muslim population increase in the state. There is a strong belief among the Assamese Hindus and tribal population that 'immigrants' would outnumber them, like in Tripura, where tribals have become a minority (Mahanta 2014). The vision document released by the BJP during the 2014 elections contained a separate section on 'North-East' with the promise to put an end to infiltration from Bangladesh (Vision Document 2014). Even during an election rally held in Silchar (a Bengali Hindu migrant-dominated constituency), on 22 February 2014, Narendra Modi as a PM contender from BJP asserted, 'There is no place of infiltrators from Bangladesh who have come to further vote bank politics agenda of others. They should be sent back. At the same time, not Assam alone but all states must accommodate Hindus coming from Bangladesh and offer them a life with dignity'. Apart from the Modi's charisma and vision for development, the party also strives to highlight the ongoing problems of illegal migration and their repatriation to Bangladesh once the party gets the power. As expected, the party could attain desired results (majority seats) in 2014 elections.

BJP'S CONSOLIDATION IN ELECTIONS 2014

The 2014 Lok Sabha elections marked a significant shift in the politics of the state. The BJP which had a negligible presence in Assam before the 2011 assembly and 2009 Lok Sabha elections could manage to defeat the Congress, that had been in power for three decades. The

BJP emerged as the single largest party in the elections. No doubt this has important implications as the party has led to the realignment of social groups in the state. Truly, 'this election has sealed the process of disintegration of the "catch-all" nature of the Congress party in Assam, the unravelling of which had already begun in 1985 when AGP won the assembly elections with a landslide victory. A major reason for this is the realignment of social groups with political parties leading to both ethnic polarization and ethnic accommodation in the state' (Saikia 2015).

The BJP's upsurge in this election had been spectacular as the party could win 7 out of 14 seats with 36.5 per cent of votes in a state which had been a Congress stronghold since Independence. For Congress, with only three seats won, this was its worst performance in the history of electoral politics in the state. The state recorded a massive voter turnout of 80 per cent, a jump of 11 per cent since 2009. The electoral outcome indicated a major shift in the political dynamics of the state. First, it brought to light a major erosion of Congress's support base, a process that had begun since Assam Movement. Second, the results also suggest an absolute decline of the AGP, polling only about 4 per cent of the total vote share. Third, one could see the phenomenal rise of the AIUDF, a party that had successfully swung the vote of the Bengali Muslim community from Congress. Fourth, and related to the first three, is the unprecedented rise of the BJP, at the cost of sharpening religious divisions in the state (Goswami and Tripathi 2015).

MAJOR ELECTORAL SHIFTS IN THE STATE

The electoral salience of 'regions within the state', that is, the nature and pattern of electoral competition in Barak Valley, Lower Assam and Upper Assam remains vital to understand the meaning of mandate. In aggregate terms, BJP got seven seats with 36 per cent vote share while Congress secured three seats with 30 per cent vote share in the 2014 elections. BJP gained 20 per cent vote share whereas Congress lost 6 per cent vote share compared to 2009 elections. AGP faced severe electoral setbacks with only 4 per cent vote share, and it retained no seats and lost 11 per cent vote share. The AIUDF won three seats, as many as the Congress did, with just 15 per cent vote share. The results, however, present a more interesting trend at regional level, wherein one could easily witness the rise of BJP in Upper Assam where the party won a 45 per cent vote share with five seats. It is in this region where the Congress received its major setback; as compared to the 2009 Lok Sabha elections, by losing three seats and only 7 per cent votes. The Congress could roughly maintain its vote share in Barak Valley and Lower Assam. The AGP also faced the same fate in Upper Assam as Congress by losing 19 per cent vote share and a seat as compared to the 2009 elections. Comparatively, AIUDF roughly remained the same across Barak Valley, Upper Assam and Lower Assam. A comparison of the 2009 and 2014 election results makes one to conclude that though BJP gained in all the three regions, its gain in Upper Assam remained most phenomenal. By looking at the local elections results in this backdrop, the trend represents its continuation and consolidation in the same manner. The BJP's dominance in Upper Assam is evident through its victory in Dibrugarh, Jorhat, Tezpur and Nagaon munici-pal elections (Rahman 2015). That the Congress not only lost Jorhat Municipal Board but also had to struggle to retain the Titabor Town Committee, the home town of the chief minister, really speaks volume on the electoral setbacks faced by Congress. BJP also held sway over Silchar in Barak Valley and Dhubri in Lower Assam. The municipal victory at Dhubri and Silchar indicates BJP's electoral stability in Lower Assam and Barak Valley. BJP's performance since 2014 election reflects upon its organizational preparedness and strategic regional alignment in recent times. Traditionally, BJP has remained strong in Barak Valley and Lower Assam in terms of vote share and seat share as compared to that in Upper Assam. Also, it always has had more vote share and seat share than the AGP during all Lok Sabha elections since 1998, while AGP has had more vote share and seat share during all Vidhan Sabha elections since 2001. The electoral stagnation witnessed by AGP and the anti-incumbency against Congress have in particular enabled inroads for the BJP in Upper Assam, a region which has most seats in Lok Sabha as well as Vidhan Sabha. An even performance by BJP across regions in Assam has been most disturbing for other parties (Table 6.2). The shift of political landscape in favour of the BJP clearly reflects upon the changing social base of the party This scenario holds potential

Table 6.2 Assam Lok Sabha Elections, 2014: Region-wise Outcome

Regions	Total Seats	Turnout (%)	Congress–BPF		BJP		AGP		AIUDF		Others		NOTA %
			Seats Won	Vote %	Seats Won	Vote %	Seats Won	Vote %	Seats Won	Vote %	Seats Won	Vote %	
Barak Valley	3	76.2	2	34.8	0	33.7	0	0.6	1	20.1	0	9.9	0.9
Lower Assam	5	82.6	0	28.8	2	29.1	0	3.6	2	18.3	1	19.5	0.7
Upper Assam	6	79.0	1	33.9	5	45.2	0	5.2	0	9.3	0	5.1	1.3
Total	14	80.1	3	31.8	7	36.5	0	3.8	3	14.8	1	12.1	1.0

Source: ECI data compiled by CSDS Data Unit.

to further weaken a party. Like AGP in particular, which has traditionally remained strong in Upper Assam. The most significant challenge
of the electoral outcome offers an explanation and understanding of
the prospects and pitfalls of AIUDF's performance. As compared to
2009, the party improved its seat tally by gaining two seats and losing
1.27 per cent vote share. Despite the fact that both Congress and
AIUDF lost their vote share, Congress still remains much evenly spread
across regions and retained salience as a major player. Congress's loss
has been most significant both in terms of vote share and seat share
in Upper Assam, while it could maintain (roughly) its vote share in
Barak Valley and Lower Assam. That in a way opens up possibilities
for Congress, based upon its regional spread, to spearhead polarization against an ascendant BJP to make its presence felt. The gain of
two seats and loss of 1.2 per cent vote share reflect upon regional
concentration of AIUDF and primarily hint at the limitation of AIUDF
in expanding its social base across regions in Assam. The AIUDF has
higher propensity to convert vote share into seat share, which is also
evident from the 2011 assembly election results. With 16 per cent vote
share AGP had 10 seats, BJP had 5 seats with 11 per cent vote share
and AIUDF had 18 with around 13 per cent vote share. However, the
major challenge before Congress remains to convert vote share into seat
share. Despite having an even regional spread, the Congress has been
posed with a stiff challenge in terms of electoral fortunes by AIUDF,
particularly in Lower Assam. The BJP in this election has managed to
consolidate the Hindu vote, both Assamese and Bengali, in large numbers. In other words, religious identity has come into sharp division as
Hindu votes are being consolidated vis-à-vis Muslim votes (Table 6.3).
Historically, whenever politics in Assam has been organized around a
singular cleavage of language or 'indigeneity', political competition has
often spiralled into 'ethnic' riots. What is clearly emerging is a form
of absolute polarization on the basis of religion, a feature that would
make Assam even more fragile.

ASSEMBLY ELECTIONS 2016

The overwhelming victory of BJP in the 2016 assembly elections began
a new phase of polarized politics in the state. Perhaps for the first time,

Table 6.3 *Voting Preference of Hindus and Muslims by Language: 2009 Lok Sabha, 2011 Assembly and 2014 Lok Sabha Elections*

	Vote for Congress (%)			Vote for BJP (%)			Vote for AIUDF (%)		
	2009	2011	2014	2009	2011	2014	2009	2011	2014
Assamese-speaking Hindus	30	38	19	23	10	63	1	1	Neg.
Bengali-speaking Hindus	45	31	27	25	42	62	2	6	Neg.
Assamese-speaking Muslims	75	59	69	9	4	4	6	15	17
Bengali-speaking Muslims	21	32	36	Neg.	1	3	78	54	45

Source: NES 2014 conducted by CSDS in Assam. Sample size 716; post-poll study 2011 conducted by CSDS in Assam, sample size 3,348; NES 2009 conducted by CSDS in Assam, sample size 1,402.

Note: The rest of the respondents voted for other parties. Data weighted by actual vote share secured of parties in each election. Neg. means Negligible.

ethnic, regional and identity-based election issues have been sidelined and questions of governance and religion played a more important position in mobilizing voters. The rise of BJP and the decimation of the Congress in 2016 in assembly elections are a few milestones on this journey. These developments had a profound impact on the politics of the state. For the first time a right wing party BJP came to power in alliance with regional and ethnic-based parties. It ended the hegemony of Congress party's rule in the state. The mandate can be seen as the voters seeking a change to end troubles, towards good governance and the development of the state. The Congress's three consecutive terms failed to show any evidence of fulfilling the above expectations. What is more significant is that the voters came out to deliver a clear mandate (Goswami 2016).

ELECTION STRATEGY

An important facet of the BJP's strategy pertains to its Hindu nationalist discourse; like in so many other states, the party has adjusted to the local variant of Hindu culture. This vernacularization process resulted in the promotion of an Assamese icon—the 15th–16th century Hindu saint and scholar, Sankardev, who had settled down in the Ahom kingdom in 1516–1517. In February 2016, Prime Minister Modi even attended the 85th conference of the Srimanta Sankardeva Sangha at Sivasagar, the erstwhile capital of the Ahom kingdom. Besides associating itself with the main Assamese Hindu figure, the BJP claimed that his legacy was under attack. It launched a campaign against the alleged occupation of Sankardev's monasteries by 'illegal immigrants'. In fact, the Bangladeshi migrants issue has been one of the cementing factors of the BJP-led coalition, as evident from the 'sons of the soil' agenda of the AGP and BPF. After all, the man the BJP projected as its candidate for chief ministership, Sarbananda Sonowal, was an AGP leader till he joined the BJP in 2011, and he had become popular after his PIL had forced the rescind of the IMDT Act of 1983. The xenophobic leanings of some Bodo sections have found expression in recurring anti-migrant violence. While the anti-immigrant discourse is not new, it took an increasingly anti-Muslim turn during the state election campaign, which Sonowal compared to 'a second battle of Saraighat', where Ahom general Lachit Borphukan defeated Mughal general Mir Jumla in 1671. The polarization along religious lines was made easier by the recent rise of the AIUDF, which had become the main Opposition party in the 2011 assembly elections.

MAINTAINING SOCIAL COALITION

The BJP set in motion the realignment process of political forces keeping in mind Assam's multi-ethnic population pattern. Riding on the apprehension over the growing insecurity of the indigenous people of Assam against the backdrop of unabated influx across the border, the BJP succeeded in manufacturing the rainbow coalition with indigenous formation and showed resilience and an ability to form alliances with regional forces like the AGP and the BPF to ensure its ascendance in the state. The seat adjustment has been well thought out since the BJP contested only 84 seats out of 126, the AGP 24 and the BPF 16. The three parties won respectively allowing the BJP to form a coalition government with its two allies. The Congress has made a seat adjustment with the United People's Front (UPF) representing indigenous communities in the state in four seats of tribal-dominated Kokrajhar Lok Sabha constituency. Although some may believe a 'Maha understanding' among the non-BJP parties would have been a plausible design to arrest the growth of the saffron party, it should be noted that the factors that made such an alliance a success in Bihar are not present in Assam. The electoral salience of 'regions within the state' primarily restrains parties from forging alliances. The third major player, the AIUDF, has allied with the JD(United) and the Rashtriya Lok Dal to cement its secular credentials. Jaffrelot (2016) also analysed an important facet of BJP's strategy pertaining to its Hindu nationalist discourse in the context of the 2016 Assam state elections. For him, 'as part of strategy, BJP has adjusted to the local variant of Hindu culture and in this vernacularization process, BJP has appropriated Sankardev, a 16th-century socioreligious reformer of Assam'. Besides, ritualistic part of religion has given added emphasis with a purpose of amplifying Hinduism, for example, Namami Brahmaputra, Namami Barak and Ambubashi Mela are enlarging its scope significantly. The BJP's strategy of intermixing local and tactical regional issues with national ones have created favourable prospect for the BJP.

VERDICT

The BJP secured 60 seats and its vote share jumped to 29.5 per cent as against five seats and 11.47 per cent votes in 2011. The Congress party, on the contrary, got a humble 26 seats with 31.2 per cent votes below its tally of 78 in the last election with a vote share of 39 per cent. The AIUDF suffered a serious setback in this election. Its tally went down to 13 from 18 in 2011 (Tables 6.4 and 6.5). Not only this, its chief Badaruddin Ajmal lost in Salmara South in Muslim-dominated Dhubri district bordering Bangladesh. The remarkable Hindu polarization around the BJP, however, is not in line with counter-consolidation

Table 6.4 *Performance in 2016 Assembly Elections, Assam*

Party	Seats Won	Vote Percentage
BJP	60	29.5
Congress (I)	26	31.0
AGP	14	8.0
AIUDF	13	13.0
BPF	12	3.9

Source: NES data CSDS.

Table 6.5 *Vote Share of Major Political Parties: 2011 Assembly, 2014 Lok Sabha and 2016 Assembly Elections*

Party	2011 Assembly	2014 Lok Sabha	2016 Assembly
BJP	11.5	36.6	29.5
AGP	16.3	3.8	8.1
BPF	6.1	2.2	3.9
Congress	39.4	29.5	31.0
AIUDF	12.6	14.8	13.0

Source: NES data CSDS.

of Muslims behind any one party. The Muslim voters did not vote en bloc. In fact, they remained as badly divided between the Congress and AIUDF as they have been for the last several elections. The AIUDF's chief campaign divided Assamese voters along communal lines. This made it easier for the BJP-led alliances to mobilize Hindu voters. Indigenous communities largely rallied behind the BJP-led alliance, considering it to a better alternative than the Congress to defeat AIUDF.

BJP's victory is unprecedented in terms of its broad geographical and social base. It is not insignificant that the BJP is in power in two of India's most sensitive states, Kashmir and Assam. This is a real test of the BJP's nation-building capacity. It settled the leadership issue. It went for a broad coalition. But most importantly, though it stuck to its policy message on immigration, the campaign was subtle and sophisticated, and less polarizing than many had feared. It injected newness by holding out the possibility of a new combination of elements: Sonowal and Sarma and Prafulla Mahanta together. Managing this combination will be a challenge; but it opens up a new vista of possibilities as well. It shows the BJP's extraordinary capacity to think politically rather than merely ideologically, when it sets its mind to it. This is something the BJP's opponents have been estimating at every stage (Mehta 2016). But this trend is also a result of decades of groundwork by the Sangh Parivar. Not only has the RSS, active in Assam since 1946, established more than 830 shakhas in the state, but other offshoots of the Parivar, including the VKA, are implementing the same welfarist strategy (free education, access to healthcare, etc.) as in other tribal belts.

PERFORMANCE AND LEADERSHIP

Performance of the government and the popularity of the chief ministerial candidate combined seemed to have influenced the electorate in the state to vote for BJP-led alliance. The survey data shows a remarkable dwindling of Tarun Gogoi's popularity as chief ministerial choice when compared to 2011. During the post-election 2016 CSDS survey, when voters were asked who they would prefer as the Chief Minister of Assam, only 25 per cent preferred Tarun Gogoi as against 38 per cent in 2011. The preference for Sarbananda Sonowal was higher (30%) than Tarun Gogoi in this election. People in the state did have a somewhat positive assessment of the Modi government. So it is reasonable to conclude that both the state government and the national government are on test when an election takes place for the state assembly. It is noteworthy that a reasonably higher proportion of the state's population are fully dissatisfied with the performance of the government than that after the last assembly elections. The percentage of partially (somewhat) satisfied with the performance of the government has also come down (Table 6.6).

Table 6.6 *Level of Satisfaction with the State Government*

Satisfaction with the State Government	2006	2011	2016
Fully satisfied	15	15	19
Somewhat satisfied	43	48	38
Somewhat dissatisfied	16	15	10
Fully dissatisfied	23	10	25
No opinion	3	11	7

Source: CSDS Data Unit.

Note: Sample size in 2006 was 2,702; in 2011 was 3,348; and in 2016 was 1,956.

Election Issues: The NES survey data reveals some interesting findings with regard to local issues of the state. It is important to know, how the voters of the state rate the Congress government on local issues of governance? The survey shows that the Congress government did not receive a fair rating. Voters' assessment on local issues such as conditions of roads, supply of electricity, drinking water, quality of education, medical facilities in governmental hospital and so on has deteriorated to a great extent than during the 2006 and 2011 elections (Table 6.7). The highest rating received for deterioration includes the supply of drinking water and medical facilities of government hospitals, followed by conditions of roads, supply of electricity and quality of education in government schools.

The Congress government could not win the support of the people even after the reduction of insurgency-related violence in the state and introduction of several social welfare schemes, as the party came to be seen by the voters as an essentially corrupt and non-performing government. Although some improvements were under way, but actual outcomes based on growth and development indicators such as unemployment, skilled education, health, rural poverty and the like presented a dismal picture. The party in power immensely failed to utilize fully centrally sponsored public funds meant for rural and urban development, communication and infrastructure development in the state. The failure of these pro-poor schemes became a great cause of concern for the poorer section of the rural as well as urban population of the state. (Goswami and Buragohain 2016). Truly, what hurts the

Table 6.7 *Assessment of the State Government on Key Issues of Governance*

Areas	2006		2011		2016	
	Improved	*Deteriorated*	*Improved*	*Deteriorated*	*Improved*	*Deteriorated*
Condition of roads	65	29	74	24	35	64
Supple of electricity	48	39	65	32	32	64
Supply of drinking water	41	43	49	45	23	73
Quality of education in government schools	49	36	59	34	40	57
Medical facilities in government hospitals	37	48	73	22	31	66

Source: Assam Assembly post-poll surveys, 2006, 2011 and 2016.

common people most was rampant corruption experienced by them in their day-to-day dealings with the administration. Corruption had eaten into the vitals of the system. News of government functionaries facing the ire of people for failing to attend to duties or for demanding bribes were becoming too common. The leadership of the Congress seemed to believe that corruption had become a non-issue as it seemed to have become a way of life. Thirsting for change of the scenario, the people were constrained to look for a change of the guard in the hope that corruption would end. Even during the survey, when voters were asked, 'In your opinion how corrupt is the Congress government in Assam—very corrupt, somewhat corrupt or not corrupt at all?', around 29 per cent replied as very corrupt, while 47 per cent as somewhat corrupt and only 12 per cent replied as not corrupt.

The community wise analysis (Table 6.8) clearly reflects BJP's success in the state has been built on an ideology that opposes the politics of statism and recognition. The consolidation of BJP across communities in the state was made possible because the party has successfully capitalized an ideological divide present in the society. On the other hand, the region-wise analysis (Table 6.9) shows that the BJP and its allies performed uniformly well in all the three regions.

2019 LOK SABHA ELECTIONS

The state has witnessed a peaceful conclusion of the 2019 polls despite the existence of a number of fractious bones of contention being carried out. Although the process of updating of the NRC had a potential of causing strife from previous elections, but the incidents of election-related violence had actually come down (*The Assam Tribune*, 2019). The BJP could eventually retain its alliance with the AGP and BPF, preserving its newly attained regional character which helped to withhold the consolidation of the anti-BJP votes, while the Opposition cast the CAB 2016 as the most significant issue, apart from projecting the failure of the BJP-led government at the Centre on various fronts during the campaign (*The Hindu* 2019). The NRC exercise in Assam had started years back during the Congress rule. But the problem is what is to be done after the implementation; deportation is obviously

Table 6.8 Dominant Community-wise Analysis: Turnout and Performance of Major Alliances and Parties, 2016

	Total Seats	Turnout	Congress		BJP+		AUDF		Other Parties	
			Won	Vote	Won	Vote	Won	Vote	Won	Vote
Overall	126	84.82	26	31.87	86	41.20	13	13.05	1	12.76
Tea-growing areas	29	84.00	4	35.51	25	50.09	0	2.55	0	10.10
Bodo	17	85.15	0	20.00	15	38.90	2	13.73	0	26.02
Muslim	40	87.49	17	34.68	13	26.99	10	27.15	0	10.52
ST	10	82.82	1	31.69	8	41.72	0	1.02	1	24.30
Others	30	82.54	4	31.62	25	54.38	1	5.89	0	7.05

Source: CSDS Data Unit.

Table 6.9 *Region-wise Analysis: Turnout and Performance of Major Alliances and Parties, 2016*

Regions	Total Seats	Turnout	[a]Congress		[b]BJP+		AUDF		Other Parties	
			Won	Vote	Won	Vote	Won	Vote	Won	Vote
Overall	126	84.82	26	31.87	86	41.20	13	13.05	1	12.76
Barak Valley	20	79.67	4	31.40	12	38.90	4	18.32	0	10.29
Lower Assam	50	86.95	12	29.06	32	39.01	6	15.90	0	0.92
Upper Assam	56	84.55	10	34.91	42	44.22	3	8.34	1	11.20

Source: CSDS Data Unit.

Notes: [a] Congress had a pre-poll alliance with UPP.
[b] BJP, AGP and BPF had a pre-poll alliance.

not an option because Bangladesh does not recognize there is outmigration. The concept of detention camps is not a way out as history is replete with such terrible exemplifications from all over the world. Therefore, bilateral negotiation with Bangladesh is considered to be the only plausible way out to address this issue. Another option is to disenfranchise those who have been proven beyond doubt to be illegal migrants. But then what happens to their children? After all, we are a signatory to the Universal Declaration of Human Rights where Articles 2, 3 and 7 are critical to this recourse (Hazarika 2016).

The NDA could remain cohesive and fought the election on three major planks: of the leadership prime minister, development initiative of the union government and the performance of the state government in Assam since 2016. By retaining the AGP and BPF, the BJP could neutralize much of the hue and cry of the Opposition over CAB that it could have faced on the election front due to its firm stand on the Bill. The popularity of the prime ministerial candidate, coupled with the satisfaction level of the voters with the performance of the union and state governments across regions and diverse social groups in the state, certainly provided an edge to the NDA. However, the social polarization along religious lines emerged as the major subtext in this election, as the divide along religion overwhelmed divisions along caste, class, language and ethnicity (Sharma and Tripathy 2019).

EFFECTS OF NATIONALISTIC SENTIMENTS

The state's publicity machinery appears to be a platform to project government's achievements real and imagined. For example, the BJP has made an effort to control the narrative after its losses in assembly elections held in December 2018. Even, the terrorist attack in Pulwama heightened nationalistic sentiments among the voters, which in turn changed the election narrative in favour of the incumbent government. It is true that for a substantial segment of voters nationalism becomes a lens to view even everyday economic issues during a national security crisis. On the other hand, it has weakened the Opposition party's plan to target government's failure to address basic issues concerning people and economic issues such as agrarian distress, unemployment and the

Rafale Scam. Elections in India are mostly about the performance of the government and Opposition's capability to convince voters about the failure of the government policies, the popularity of leaders and the ability of the organizational machinery to reach out different social groups for making effective coalition. The 2019 verdict appeared to be a sum total of competitive credibility on all these factors.

ILLEGAL MIGRATION ISSUE

Illegal migration from Bangladesh into India is substantial but there are other interlocking issues that call for attention. First comes the scale of migration. Most of the figures are simply assertions and the analysis is based on assumptions. The other is the impact that such perceptions are prevalent not just in eastern India, especially in Assam and West Bengal, but also across the country, with antipathy growing against Muslims of Bangla origin. As far as numbers are concerned, the truth is that decades after anti-Bangladeshi campaign began in the late 1970s, few have been detected and deported despite many promises. Not even the Centre has a clear idea of how many illegal migrants are in India, not just Assam. For years there has been a sense of fatigue in Assam. Thus Prime Minister Modi correctly chose statesmanship over local politics by settling the Indo-Bangladesh land boundary issue, a problem that had been unresolved for decades. That way, he piquantly created a challenge for the Assam unit of his own party which had opposed the deal, claiming it would increase illegal migration (Hazarika 2019).

However, the complexity has deepened by sweeping media reports which posit a future where 'Bangladeshi Muslims' will be a majority in the state and ignore the fact that it has three major groups of Muslims (Assamese-speaking Muslims whose ancestors date back to the 13th century, Muslims of Bangla origin, many of whose ancestors came over 100 years ago, and the post-1971 Bangladeshi Muslims). Indeed this last group is also conveniently forgotten: those who moved from East Pakistan before 1971 are not Bangladeshis. Also ignored is the fact that there is a high fertility rate among Muslim groups in Western Assam where large families are the norm. This is a key factor in demographics, especially if one considers the fact that Assam has smaller border with Bangladesh than Meghalaya, Mizoram, Tripura or West Bengal. There is hostility to migration in Assam and the Northeast. Most migrants seek safe haven. In addition to that, there is a greater economic security as Bangladesh's economy has grown making outmigration risky and less attractive. The combination of selective facts, selective memory and rhetoric can be a deadly combination as seen in 2012 after the incidents in Western Assam where both Bodo and Muslims were victims. Hate-mongering triggered an exodus of lakhs of workers from the region. The incident in February 1983 in the state should suffice as an adequate warning about vulnerability of this region (Hazarika 2016).

CITIZENSHIP ISSUE

By ignoring the ethnic plurality of the state population, the BJP has tried to create through the CAB an affinity towards Hindu identity. It served its purpose towards creating a 'Hindu Rashtra' with the introduction of CAB in the Lower House of Parliament in 2016. The CAB was introduced to allow non-Muslim illegal immigrants from Bangladesh, Pakistan and Afghanistan to gain citizenship. For the party, CAB is the only solution to save Assam from Muslim infiltrators and if the state does not provide space to Hindu Bengalis, then Assam will soon become a Muslim-dominated state. This position is clear in Amit Shah's statement where he affirmed, 'The way demography is changing in Assam, without the Citizenship Bill, the people of the state will be in big danger' (Press Trust of India 2019). Noted Nobel Laureate Amartya Sen while commenting on the CAB remarked, 'The Citizenship Bill and the National Register of Citizens (NRC) are discriminatory. The regulations being advocated and adopted have a lot of discrimination, particularly on the grounds of religion, which in my judgement is against the spirit of the Constitution.' Massive public outrage has been noted throughout Assam and the rest of the northeast region against the Centre's move to grant Indian citizenship to Hindu Bangladeshis by bringing an amendment to the Citizenship Act, 1955.

The party's emphasis on the illegal migration issue continued in the 2019 elections. The party manifesto thus stated:

> There has been a huge change in the cultural and linguistic identity of some areas due to illegal immigration, resulting in an adverse impact on local people's livelihood and employment. We will expeditiously complete the National Register of Citizens process in these areas on priority. In future we will implement the NRC in a phased manner in other parts of the country. (Election Manifesto, Bharatiya Janata Party 2019).

Its commitment to bring the CAB if voted to power was also mentioned. However, the BJP has crafted its election campaign so strategically that it did not harm the sentiments of the people. For example, the election campaign strategy was different in Brahmaputra Valley region from that of the Barak Valley. While in their campaign rally in the Brahmaputra Valley, BJP President Amit Shah and Prime Minister Narendra Modi didn't make any comment on the Bill. However, in his first campaign speech in the Barak Valley, PM Narendra Modi mentioned about the Bill stating, 'We will take care of the sentiments of Assamese communities before reintroducing the bill so that no one is hurt. The bill will be tabled and passed after thorough discussions with all stakeholders in Assam.'

ELECTION VERDICT

The Lok Sabha elections to Assam held in 2019 seemed to represent continuity with the political consolidation of the BJP that was witnessed in the 2016 assembly elections. The BJP's ability to craft a social coalition with the leadership of diverse ethnic groups and forge electoral alliances with prominent regional players like the AGP and BPF in 2016 proved to be a master stroke leading to the formation of the first ever BJP-led government in the state. The major challenge during the Lok Sabha elections before the BJP in Assam was the perpetuation of the social base that had shifted to the party during the assembly elections of 2016. In part, it remained contingent upon the party's ability to keep intact its alliance with the AGP and BPF (Kalita 2019). The BJP could eventually retain its alliance with the AGP and BPF, preserving its newly attained regional character which helped to withhold the consolidation of the anti-BJP votes, while the Opposition cast the CAB, 2016, as the most significant issue, apart from projecting the failure of the BJP-led government at the Centre on various fronts during the campaign (*The Hindu* 2019).

The BJP won 9 out of the 10 seats it contested. The Congress won three seats (same as in 2014). Traditionally, the Congress in Assam had been the catch-all party with an even spread of vote share across regions and social classes. However, a major challenge before Congress in Assam remains the conversion of votes into seats. This election was no exception and the party witnessed an increase in its vote share. This happened primarily because of two reasons. First, the AIUDF contested elections only on three seats and, thus, the Congress could get the anti-BJP votes in all other seats left by the AIUDF. Second, the increase in vote share is also because the party contested alone on all the 14 seats. The AIUDF, contesting on three seats, could win only the Dhubri seat, which was retained by the party's president, Badruddin Ajmal. The AIUDF suffered a loss of two seats as compared to 2014. The decline happened as a significant share of traditional voters of the AIUDF shifted to the Congress this time, even in the constituencies that the AIUDF contested. It is evident as a proportionately large number of Bengali-speaking Muslim voters voted for the Congress in this election.

RETAINING THE SOCIAL BASE

The survey indicates that the NDA could secure votes from all social groups evenly, barring the Muslim voters who predominantly favoured the Congress (Table 6.10). The traditional Congress support base, comprising the tea-tribe workers, Muslims and ST voters appears to have suffered a split, as the BJP has been able to attract tea workers and STs as its new social base since 2014 (Sharma 2014). The phenomenal performance of the BJP in Upper Assam constituencies of Lakhimpur, Dibrugarh, Jorhat and Tezpur, along with the Autonomous District seat in Barak Valley, remains the by product of the tribal and Adivasi shift of support to the BJP. In all the five constituencies, the tea workers and STs constitute a significant part of the voting population. The

Table 6.10 *Vote in Percentage by Different Social Groups: 2019 Lok Sabha Elections, Assam*

Social Groups	Congress	NDA	AIUDF	Others	n
Upper Caste	13	74	–	12	101
OBC	22	60	–	18	260
Dalit	9	66	–	26	58
Adivasi	7	86	–	7	112
Hindu	16	70	Less than 1	14	694
Muslim	70	7	20	3	397

Source: CSDS Data Unit; CSDS-Assam Pradesh NES post-poll survey 2019.

Note: Figures in percentage (except *n*) and may not add up to 100 due to rounding off; weighted data set (*n* = 1121).

BJP fielded three candidates belonging to the Adivasi community from Dibrugarh, Tezpur and Karimganj, and all of them won their respective seats. Apart from these constituencies, the Adivasi and ST population remains dispersed in other constituencies too and their shift to the BJP has considerably strengthened the party's dominance in Assam. However, the Kokrajhar Lok Sabha seat, having significant tribal population, marked an exception to the BJP's dominance over seats. Naba Sarania, an independent candidate, could retain this ST seat. Sarania's win can be attributed to non-tribal support, especially from Muslims under the influence of All Bodoland Minority Students' Union (ABMSU) that openly supported him, along with a considerable proportion of non-tribal Hindus, including the non-Bodo tribes. The consolidation over Adivasi and ST votes, coupled with the huge shift of caste Hindu voters towards the NDA, enabled its even performance across regions (Table 6.11). The BJP's alliance with the AGP was central to its forging a caste Hindu consolidation towards the NDA (Sharma and Tripathi 2019).

REGION-WISE VOTING PATTERN

The region-wise analysis of the voting pattern in the state reflects a noticeable trend. A significant shift of the tea community, caste Hindu

Table 6.11 *Region-wise Vote and Seat Distribution*

Region	Total Seats	INC		NDA		AIUDF		Others	
		Seats Won	Vote (%)	Seats Won	Vote (%)	Seats Won	Vote (%)	Seats Won	Vote (%)
Barak Valley	3	0	25.88	3	51.52	0	16.54	0	6.06
Lower Assam	5	1	32.24	2	33.56	1	12.26	1	21.94
Upper Assam	6	2	42.18	4	53.08	0	0	0	4.74
Overall	14	3	35.44	9	44.28	1	7.8	1	12.45

Source: CSDS survey data.

and ST communities to BJP from Congress has attributed to the BJP's success in the state. Table 6.11 shows the complete dominance of the BJP in the Barak Valley region. In Barak Valley constituencies, the introduction of CAB has helped in consolidating the Hindu votes. The Barak Valley, with its large migrant and indigenous Bengali-speaking population could have delivered an anti-BJP mandate. This, however, did not happen. The CAB, devised to appease the Hindu Bengalis, may have polarized the voters along religious lines. This can be inferred from the huge increase in BJP's votes in Silchar. The party had succeeded in its strategy to neutralize the opposition to the CAB and could divert the attention of Hindus towards the increase of Muslim population. In the Brahmaputra Valley region, the intensely debated CAB, however, did not harm the electoral prospect of the BJP in Lok Sabha elections. The tea-community voters play an important role in this region. Prior to the 2014 elections, Upper Assam used to be a Congress bastion. However, since the 2014 Lok Sabha elections, the shifting of votes towards BJP is apparent.

The CSDS survey data of 2019 elections clearly reveal the fact that polarization was found to be most acute in the states where the proportions of Muslims is high, namely Assam, UP, West Bengal and Bihar. Not only did the BJP get a massive proportion of Hindu votes in these states, this share was much larger than what it received in the

2014 elections. Increased Hindu support for the BJP in the states (and elsewhere too) ended up rendering Muslim consolidation behind the Congress and other Opposition parties ineffective again (*The Hindu* 2019).

The 2019 elections were held against the backdrop of massive protests over the CAB, 2016 that seeks to bestow citizenship upon certain categories of non-Muslim migrants escaping religious persecution in neighbouring Muslim-majority countries, including Bangladesh, was seen as a litmus test for the BJP. The party's advocacy in favour of the bill was expected to pose a major challenge to it in terms of retaining its base among the state's indigenous communities that were bitterly opposed to the Bill on the grounds that it would lead to an influx of persecuted refugees from neighbouring Bangladesh. While regionalist sentiments were against any further influx of foreigners in the region, organizations representing local Muslim populations also opposed the bill as it sought to discriminate between migrants on religious grounds. The BJP's success lied in its ability to neutralize the opposition to the controversial bill among non-Muslims, diverting attention towards the increase in the percentage of Muslim population in the state, presumably due to an unabated influx from Bangladesh with the patronage of the Congress. This marked a continuation of the trend witnessed in the 2016 assembly elections when it managed to patch up a 'rainbow coalition' with regionalist groups, raising the issue of protection of *jati, mati, bheti* (community, land and homestead) from 'illegal Bangladeshi Muslim migrants', and drawing support from diverse ethnic communities with its promise of freeing the land from the foreigners' clutches. The 2019 Lok Sabha poll marked a sharpening trend towards polarization, with the AIUDF's decision not to field candidates against the Congress in all but three constituencies being interpreted by the BJP as an open consolidation of Muslim voters in favour of the Congress. The upsurge of the BJP, a party representing Hindu nationalism at the national level, in a state that has traditionally witnessed the dominance of ethnic politics based on linguistic and tribal identities marks the trend towards religious consolidation, where the issue of illegal immigration from across the international border emerged as a crucial point of religious polarization. The strategy of polarization has brought electoral divident to the BJP in Assam. But this trend is also a result of decades of groundwork by the Sangh Parivar. The NRC of 1950 could be the best immediate protection for Assam to 'provide constitutional, legislative and administrative safeguards for cultural, social, linguistic identity' to the Assamese people. However, it is to be remembered that entitlements that come with citizenship if denied to certain sections of society, it effectively pushes those communities out of the consensus-building process that is required for democracy. The sooner people's voices are heard with due seriousness and addressed democratically the better it is for the state as well as the nation. BJP's ideological objection to a review of the Armed Forces (Special Powers) Act and the sedition law symbolizes increasing legitimacy of the idea of a strong militarist state. Theoretically, this idea is poised on limiting the scope of what constitutes citizenship and, in practice, it tends to convert citizen into a subject by restricting freedoms.

CONCLUSION

With the electoral victory of the BJP-led NDA, voters might now feel the end of the troubles and the beginning of the politics of good governance and development. However, such a reading might be a premature one and would be a triumph of hope over reality. The party won due to combination of many factors, the strategy of getting a once powerful entity like the AGP to become an ally blunted much of the reluctance of a segment of indigenous people to vote for the party, with hopes being roused once again of a permanent solution to the foreign infiltration issue despite its failure in the last two years to take steps at resolving it. This particular issue became so prominent than all other issues, such as the Land Swap Deal with Bangladesh, the notification of granting refugee status to Hindu Bangladeshis, the Centre's denial to grant ST status to six communities and the union government's determination to resume the construction of the Subansiri Lower Hydroelectric Project (SLHEP), around which the resentment against the than government had gradually been building, were suddenly pushed to the periphery.

The latest NRC in Assam is a Supreme Court-mandated and -monitored process. But the incumbent party in the state is itself up in arms against it, and wants it done all over again. Thus, it is a clear fallout of the political obsession with the NRC in Assam that calls for the implementation of similar exercises elsewhere in the country to weed out illegal Bangladeshi migrants. But the anti-Bangladeshi sentiment morphed into anti-Bengali prejudice. When politicians whip up ethnic passions in a diverse society, emotions override logic. What is interesting, there is no clarity on what happens after identification and prosecution: as they cannot be deported for as no such protocols exist between India and Bangladesh. The Bill has already triggered divisions most visibly between Asomiya-dominated Brahmaputra Valley and Bengali-dominated Surma Valley. The exercise has caused tremendous hardship and harassment for crores of people. It is also a fact that no country or state can remain unconcerned with such a large influx of illegal migrants.

The big question that arises is whether the BJP has the confidence to bank on the development card, or its ideological instincts reassert itself again? One has to wait and see. Given the nature of diversity in the state in terms of ethnic, linguistic, cultural and religious pluralism, dealing with the citizenship issue solely by acknowledging the exclusivity of identity based on religion would be counterproductive to the democratic, socialist and secular basis of the nation. Rather than resolving this contentious issue through democratic ways, such hasty and improper decisions of great public concern might further complicate the situation causing more resentment and distrust. For all these deleterious effects of the Bill, the people of the region seemed to have voiced strongly against it. It is beyond comprehension of the masses as to why the government is so enthusiastic to pass such a controversial Bill by flouting the basic norms and procedures and disregarding popular resentment. A right-based approach, girded by law, holding Article 21 high, guided by common sense and sympathy—rather than abuse and prejudice—must win the day (Hazarika 2018). Already the NDA led government in Assam has entered the last year of its term in the state. However, it is not easy to opine that the troubled state has recovered from its inherent structural difficulties. The state can recover only if it adheres to the principles of true federalism with a commitment to constitutional procedures.

Finally, what does this historic mandate mean for the trajectory of Indian democracy? As much as the 2019 election shows signs of a deepening and maturing of the democratic process, it also carries a possibility of India becoming a democracy with majoritarian sensibilities. The Idea of India, as Sunil Khilnani wrote, is a celebration of Ideas of India. Only magnanimity towards ideological adversaries and tolerance of dissent can bring to fruition Modi's new idea of *sabka vishwas* (Verma 2019).

REFERENCES

Bharatiya Janata Party, 2019. Sankalp Patra [Election manifesto], Lok Sabha Election, New Delhi, 11. Available at: http//www.bjp.org/en/manifesto2019

Bhattacharjee, Malini. 2016. 'Tracing the Emergence and Consolidation of Hindutva in Assam'. *Economic & Political Weekly* 51 (17): 80–87.

Chandhoke, Neera. 2014. 'India 2014: Return of the One-Party Dominant System'. Istituto Affari Internazionali. Available at: www.jstor.org/stable/resrep09761

Goswami, Sandhya. 2012. 'Changing Trends of Electoral Politics'. *Seminar* 640 (December). Available at: https://www.india-seminar.com/2012/640/640_sandhya_goswami.htm

———. 2016. 'Winds of Change in Assam'. *Deccan Herald*, 22 May.

Goswami, Sandhya and Dikshita Buragohain. 2017. 'Democracy and Governance: Assam State Assembly Elections 2016'. *Journal of Political Science* IX: 19–25.

Goswami, Sandhya, and Vikas Tripathi. 2015. 'Understanding the Political Shift in Assam: Withering Congress Dominance'. *Economic & Political Weekly* 50 (39): 67–71.

Hasan, Zoya. 1990. 'Changing Orientation of the State and the Emergence of Majoritarianism in the 1980s'. *Social Scientist* 18 (8–9, August–September): 27–37.

Hazarika, Sanjoy. 2016. 'Assam's Minority Report'. *The Times of India*, 12 January.

———. 2018. 'Defining Citizenship: Assam on the Edge Again'. *Economic & Political Weekly* 30 (28 July): 12–13.

Hibbard, Scott W. 2010. *Religious Politics and Secular States: Egypt, India, and the United States*. Baltimore, MD: The Johns Hopkins University Press.

Jaffrelot, Christophe. 2015. *Hindu Nationalism: A Reader*. New Delhi: Permanent Black.

———. 2016. 'BJP's Assam Win Is Proof Hindutva Has Reached Areas Where It Was Marginal'. *The Indian Express*, 11 June. Available at: http://indianexpress.com

com/article/opinion/columns/bjpsarbananda-sonowal-assam-assembly-elections-tarun-gogoi-congress-the-enigma-of-arrival–2846193/

Kalita, Prabin. 2019. 'AGP Quits NDA as Cabinet Approves Citizenship Bill'. *The Times of India*, 8 January.

Kanungo, Pralay. 2011. 'Casting Community, Culture and Faith: Hindutva's Entrenchment in Arunachal Pradesh'. In Cultural Entrenchment of Hindutva: Local Mediations and Forms of Convergence, edited by D. Berti, N. Jaoul, and P. Kanungo, 91–117. New Delhi: Routledge.

Mahanta, Nani Gopal. 2014. 'Lok Sabha Elections in Assam Shifting of Traditional Vote Bases to BJP'. *Economic & Political Weekly* 49 (35): 19–22.

Palshikar, Suhas. 2019. 'People's Demand for a Strong Leader Feeds into the BJP's Majoritarian Politics Perfectly'. *The Indian Express*, 26 June.

Press Trust of India. 2019. 'BJP Won't Let Assam Become Another Kashmir, Sacrifices of Jawans in Pulwama Won't Go in Vain: Amit Shah'. *Firstpost*, 17 February. Available at: https://www.firstpost.com/politics/bjp-wont-let-assam-become-another-kashmir-sacrifices-of-jawans-in-pulwama-wont-go-in-vain-amit-shah–6102601.html

Rahman, Wasim. 2015. 'Cong Loses Board in Gogoi Citadel'. *The Telegraph*, 13 February.

Saikia, Smitana. 2015. 'General Election 2014: Will BJP's Gains Polarize Assam Further?' *Studies in Indian Politics* 3 (1): 69–80.

Sharma, Dhruba Pratim. 2014. 'Saffron Surge in Assam'. *Research Journal Social Sciences* 22 (2): 224–233.

Sharma, Dhruba Pratim, and Vikas Tripathi. 2019. 'Assam 2019 NDA Deepens Its Dominance'. *Economic & Political Weekly* 54 (34): 23–25.

The Assam Tribune. 2019. 'Democratic Ethos', 1 May.

The Hindu. 2019. '2019 Lok Sabha Election: BJP–AGP Alliance Back on Track in Assam', 13 March.

Verma, Rahul. 2019. 'The Problem'. *Seminar* 720 (August). Available at: https://www.india-seminar.com/2019/720/720_the_problem.htm

Challenges Ahead

Assam has undergone two significant alterations in its political contours since the 1980s: one leading to the rise of a regional party AGP and the other leading to a firm foothold by the BJP. The challenge to the Congress in the state mainly came from the educated urban middle class, who took the lead in the Assam Movement. Towards the end of the 1970s, the indigenous people of Assam led by AASU and the AGSP started the Assam Movement to protest against the threat posed by unabated illegal infiltration of people from Bangladesh into the Northeast in general and Assam in particular. The Assam Movement demonstrated the strength of regional identities in the state, and it gained momentum in the first half of the 1980s that continued till 1985. The Congress party was in power then and was instrumental in abetting and exacerbating the problem caused by illegal migration issue. The movement gave expression to the rise of Assamese nationalism and at the same time stimulated various subregional and ethnic aspirations. The Assam Movement was finally resulted in the formation of a regional party, AGP which challenged the dominance of the Congress in the state in 1985 election.

The 1985 election was a 'critical' or 'realigning' election that changed the structure of political competition of Assam. The ground for this electoral realignment was prepared by the Assam Movement that brought considerable changes in the support structure and issue articulation of political parties in Assam. Two fundamental changes are noticed: a 'fragmentation' of party's political space and an explosion of ethnicities in the arena of politics of the state. With this election, the Congress system in Assam gave way to a multi-party system in which political parties of various ethnic groups or smaller cultural communities began to play significant role in the politics of the state. This transition from a party that shaped the politics of the country to a party now shaped by politics around it has been rather difficult and painful for the Congress. The AGP did emerge not only as the main rival of the Congress but it also appeared to have pushed the national Opposition parties to the sidelines. With the defeat of Congress, the party system in Assam has changed from a single-party dominance to a truly multi-party system that shows high degree of party fragmentation. The slow and somewhat dormant process of politicization of ethnicities has suddenly gained momentum. The intensity of electoral competition has increased with the rise in electoral volatility. This has been accompanied by a participatory upsurge. The period beginning with the AGP is characterized by simultaneous operation of multiple and competing ideological axes, which shows the emergence and institutionalization of an intense competitive politics in the state, in which three or more political parties have entrenched themselves in electoral competition. The multipolar competition has ensured more space for smaller formations and interests. However, the rise of multipolar competition is associated with sharp antagonisms with social fragmentations enduring ethnicization of politics. New social and cultural identities have asserted themselves by changing the established contours of the party system in the state leading to fresh alignments. The Left parties faced a steady political decline primarily because of their opposition to the Assam Movement and have been forced to accept the reality of the regional forces. The BJP has entered as an important electoral force in the decade but more as a sectarian than as a nationalist force. These developments profoundly impacted on the politics of the state. The entry of new social groups and parties bears the potential of giving more meaning to competitive democracy. Yet greater number of parties has not necessarily meant more and better choices and better policies. Elected governments have repeatedly failed to translate popular support into effective policies. The advantage secured by the AGP as a result of historical and political exigencies to unite the people for forming a cohesive Assamese nationality could not be capitalized by the party. It is now universally acknowledged that the party has failed to fulfil its historic role. The AGP began to face trouble from within its own ranks almost from the moment the leaders assumed political office. The party's inability to adopt a clear-cut stand on its electoral alliance strategies since its emergence as a political force in Assam is a clear failure on its part. More it left the coalition with the BJP in 2019 during the earlier turmoil over its opposition to what was then the CAB. When the Bill did not pass in the Rajya Sabha and fresh elections were announced, the party promptly came back into the saddle with the ruling party. It came back to the same coalition government that it had earlier opposed. What is worst, the lone AGP MP in the Rajya Sabha voted for the Bill that turned it in to an Act of Parliament even as the AGP joined a clutch of petitions, including the Congress and AASU's Union from which regional party was emerged, challenging this very Act. Time and again, at the decisive moments, an uncertain and divided AGP has failed to show any integrity or act firmly. In successive polls, the party joined hands with different parties, including the Left and the rightists, to the detriment of its own image as a regional party with a highly variegated multi-ethnic electoral base. The lack of ideology, failure to address the basic issues on which the party was formed, along with opportunism and factionalism within the party, were some of the factors that contributed to the defeat of AGP in the election. Besides, regionalism as an ideology is no more an exclusive domain, with the Congress and, more recently, the BJP making inroads into its support base. Defection is one issue which is quite strong within the AGP. Many leaders left the party or turned against it on the eve of elections or during submission of nomination papers. Many veteran party leaders, activists and sitting legislators Left the party, aghast at the lack of tickets for them and some even contested as rebels or independent candidates. Those failing to get candidature did not even hesitate to indulge in vandalism in the party office. Such behaviour certainly weakened the image of the party and exposed the lack of discipline and democracy within the party organization. Besides, the party failed to build on the failure of the Congress government to adequately address major issues concerning the state such as foreign nationals issue, floods, soil erosion, impact of big dams, corruption, problems of diverse ethnic minorities and others. The AGP's sole mobilization plank revolved only around the institutionalization of corruption within the Congress party and government. In reality, the issue of corruption did not sway the general public beyond a few based in urban locations. Today, the AGP is in a state of disarray without the regional clout it once had, in providing an alternative to 'national parties'. The failure of the AGP to address the main issue of illegal migration on which the party owed its origin appears to be a disgrace on the efficacy of the regional force touted as a viable remedy for political stability in the state.

CONGRESS DECLINE

With the empathetic return of the Congress in post-Congress era, it might be tempting to conclude that things are back to where they were before the Assam Movement that shook the political framework of the state. But nothing could be further from reality. The political stagnation that marked AGP politics led to subsequent revival of the Congress in the state as the most dominant player. The three successive electoral victories for the Congress are a testimony to this. However, Congress now is radically different from the Congress of the Congress system. It is no longer an umbrella organization that covers all the various ethnicities and communities of the state. The decline of Congress is the result of the inevitable logic of competitive politics. The organizational linkage between top leaders of the party with the voters seemed to have eroded. Moreover, as the crisis of the political economy developed since the 1970s, the party suffered a deficit of social bases. The Congress in the state is principally dependent on the support of the Muslims and other ethnic minorities. However, despite the widespread disillusionment with the AGP, the Congress is yet to win back the trust of the dominant Assamese community that used to be the mainstay of the Congress in the state. Unlike most other states, the Congress is not the most favoured party of the STs. No wonder, the party does not enjoy the kind of hegemony it had in the pre-1978 days. In that sense, the return of the Congress in the late 90s shows how far the state has travelled from the days of the Congress system. The moot point is not the defeat of the Congress in 1978 but its recovery from such defeats all over the country. It was the anti-foreigners' movement from 1979 to 1985 that transformed the nature of political alignment of the state. The short-term consequence was the fall of Congress and the rise of the AGP as the carrier of the Assamese nationalism. Although the AGP did not succeed, unlike some parties like AIDMK in Tamil Nadu, in consolidating its political position and emerging as the stable alternative, the party system in the state underwent a long-term change. Actually the Assam movement has started the processes of ethnicization of politics and political fragmentation. Since then a number of regional and subregional parties have emerged as an important political force in the state. Assam's multi-ethnic and polycultural reality added a peculiar dimension to this trend as most of these parties are based on one or the other ethnic group. This phenomenon is not confined to the regional and subregional parties alone. The national parties have also gone through the process of ethnicization. The decline of Congress has been met by two important political developments: the growing significance of regional and ethnic parties like BPF and AIUDF, and the rise of BJP. The AUDF was formed in reaction to the perceived apathy of the Congress towards the minorities. Since the main issue that has dominated the politics of the state is the concern for identity, the Congress and the BJP have also sought to mobilize a few sections. Yet to describe the change in the state politics as a journey from 'catch-all' party system to political and ethnic fragmentation does not do full justice to the complexities of ethnicity politics that has dominated the electoral arena in the last two decades. The transformation in Assam is better seen as a reconfiguration that involves multiple realignments. It includes the familiar and standard story of the renegotiation of political loyalties by the existing social groups. The disillusionment of the Assamese middle class with the Congress and with search for a political vehicle for their aspirations is illustrative of this process. The changing voting preference of the Muslims across the various elections constitutes another instance of the same process of electoral realignment. This standard story does not recognize another kind of realignment that has taken place simultaneously. The state has also witnessed the reworking of the boundaries of social communities themselves or a redrawing of the politically active social cleavages. Competitive politics creates and recreates imagined communities. The political salience of the various divisions within the Muslims or the rise of a large number of hitherto unknown tribal groups illustrates this process. Electoral competition has mobilized many formerly passive socio-economic groups and brought them into the political arena. Assam politics illustrates during this period a realignment in the relationship among various kinds of pre-existing social cleavages; for instance, between religion and migration or between language or tribes and region. The simultaneous operation of these realignments has made contemporary Assam into a virtual laboratory of politics of ethnicity.

A PARADIGM SHIFT

A paradigm shift in the politics of the state is apparent since the 2014 Lok Sabha elections. In 2016 assembly elections, the BJP registered a historic victory in the state and politics has entered a new era of Hindu nationalist hegemony fuelled by Modi's extraordinary popularity. The BJP has successfully capitalized on an ideological divide present in the society. Religion provides moral framework under which modern politics functions. Religion is vital to the construction of collective and particularly national identities. The emergence of the AIUDF is particularly significant for a party like the BJP which has been effectively playing the anti-Muslim card in Assam. For most Hindus in Assam, the fear of being overpowered by a larger Muslim community has concretized in the shape of AIUDF that became the main Opposition party in the state in 2011. With the emergence of a Muslim-majority party, the prospect of polarization in the state in terms of religion has sharpened. This in turn has provided a favourable climate for Hindutva politics to operate. Besides, the crafting of a new social coalition based upon the primacy of regional subtext by the BJP is an important explanation for its unprecedented performance. On the hand, other Congress party lost its pre-eminence since 2014 elections due to the communal polarization followed by BJP and AIUDF. As a result, its position further declined in subsequent elections. Although the party continues to have a geographical space available throughout the state, its sociopolitical space has declined. The party still has a sizeable presence in terms of vote share and a political position as the main Opposition party, but it does not have a sharp social profile nor it could come out with any social character or identity. The Adivasi votes are getting divided between BJP and Congress. Muslim votes are also moving away from Congress. These limitations of the absence of social space for the party are both cause and effect of the absence of political space in the state.

The BJP in the state has emerged as the principal carrier of majoritarian idea. However, the BJP has not followed the same trajectory to propagate majoritarian ideology in the state as in the rest of the states in India. By moving away from its standard techniques of mobilizing support, it instead has focused on adapting local cults and symbols. Apart from this, the party could consolidate its presence by involving itself in various welfare services. Even BJP's campaign strategy has realigned specifically to situate itself on a regional orbit. The party also demonstrated its ability for flexibility aimed totally at electoral gains. Politics of indigeneity and consequent polarization induced the emergence of religious identity as the major determinant of electoral choice. The greater salience of religion as compared to language and ethnicity has a casting impact over electoral mobilization and electoral choice. An exclusive religious politics followed by the party no doubt, propelled it to power and popularity in the state even beyond expectation, but it does not provide a viable basis for governance. The long-standing vital issues related to immigration, land and identity since the pre-partition days have remained unaddressed. Moreover, the prevailing political scenario in the state today is riddled with popular dissension, public resentment over the Citizenship Act; the divisive policies in handling major ethnic issues and failure to provide livelihood and employment to the needy ones speak volumes about its inability to come up to the popular expectation. History does not repeat itself. But it does rhyme. We can find the rhymes today.

FURTHER READINGS

Barooah, Nirode K. 2010. *Gopinath Bordoloi, 'The Assam Problem' and Nehru's Centre*. Guwahati: Bhabani Print and Publications.

Barua, Sandhya. 1974. 'Language Problem in Assam'. *Social Scientist* 6: 66–78.

Baruah, Joydeep. 2009. 'Egoistic Alliance sans Real Politics'. *The Assam Tribune*, 24 May.

Baruah, Sanjib. 2001. *India against Itself: Assam and Politics of Nationality*. New York, NY: Oxford University Press.

Baruah, Sanjib. 2011. 'Assam, Don't Hold Your Breath'. *The Times of India*, 2 May.

Bezbaruah, M. P. 2016. 'The Muslim Factor in Assam's Election'. NDTV, 1 April.

Bhambri, C P. 2018. *Understanding Indian Politics*. New Delhi: Shipra Publications.

Borah, Jnanashree, and Sandhya Goswami. 2016. 'Social Exclusion and the Tea Tribe Communities: Experiences from Assam'. In *Ethnicity and Political Economy in Northeast India*, edited by H. Srikanth and Rooplekha Borgohain, 181–94. Guwahati: DVS Publishers.

Chaudhari, K. 2001. 'An Alliance of Convenience'. *Frontline*, 27 April.

Chibber, Pradeep K., and Rahul Verma. 2018. *Ideology and Identity: The Changing Party Systems of India*. New Delhi: Oxford University Press.

Choudhery, D. R. 2009. 'Assam Politics: Rise of AUDF as a Major Force'. *The Assam Tribune*, 24 May.

Dainik Asom, 6 February 1998.

Das, B. M. 2011. *The People of Assam: Origin and Composition*. New Delhi: Gyan Books.

Das, H. N. 2011. 'Challenges before Tarun Gogoi'. *The Assam Tribune*, 17 May.

Das, B. M. 2011. *The People of Assam: Origin and Composition*. New Delhi: Gyan Books.

Dasgupta, Jyotirindra. 1998. 'Community, Authenticity and Autonomy: Insurgence and Institutional Development in India's North-East'. In *Community Conflicts and the State in India*, edited by Amrita Basu and Atul Kohli, 183–214. New Delhi: Oxford University Press.

Dutta, A. 2011. 'Gostigoto Danda' (in Assamese) (Communal conflict). *Dainik Janambhumi*, 13 January.

Dutta, Akhil Ranjan. 2014. 'BJP's Consolidation, AIUDF's Polarisation, and Congress' Defeat in Assam'. In *India's 2014 Elections: A Modi-Led BJP Sweep*, edited by P. Wallace, 381–403. New Delhi: SAGE Publications.

Dwaipayan. 2009. 'Poll Prospects of Three Fronts in Assam'. *The Assam Tribune*, 3 April.

Gohain, Hiren. 1996. 'Extremist Challenge and the Indian State: Case of Assam. *Economic & Political Weekly* 31 (31, 3 August).

Goswami, Dulal C., and Partha J. Das. 2003. 'The Brahmaputra River, India: The Eco-hydrological Context of Water Use in One of the World's Most Unique River Systems'. *Ecologist Asia*. Special issue on *Large Dams in Northeast India: River, Forests, People and Power* 11 (1, January–March): 9–14.

Goswami, Sandhya. 1995. 'Population Migration and Its Impact on Assam's Economic and Social Milieu'. *Journal of Political Science*, 1: 69–78.

———, ed. 2015. *Troubled Diversity: The Political Process in Northeast India*. New Delhi: Oxford University Press.

Hasan, Zoya. 2012. *Congress After Indira: Policy, Power, political Change (1984–2009)*. New Delhi: Oxford University Press.

Hussain, Monirul. 1993. *The Assam Movement: Class, Ideology and Identity*. New Delhi: Manak Publications.

Hussain, Sazza. 2011. 'Assembly Polls and Assam Muslims'. *The Assam Tribune*, 26 March.

Kalita, Prabin. 2009. 'Congress Backs Ismail to Checkmate Ajmal'. *The Times of India*, 23 May.

Kar, R. K. 1999. 'A Panoramic View of the Tea and Ex-tea Tribes of Assam'. In *Identity of Adivasis in Assam*, edited by T. Pulloppillil, 21–46. New Delhi: Indian Publishers Distributors.

Lokniti–CSDS Team. 2009. 'How India Voted: Verdict 2009'. *The Hindu*, 26 May.

Mahanta, N. 2011. 'Mandate 2011: A Political Analysis'. *The Assam Tribune*, 2 June.

Majumdar, R. C. 1988. 'British Paramountcy and Indian Renaissance'. Part 1, Vol. 9 of *The History and Culture of the Indian People*. Bombay: Bharatiya Vidya Bhavan.

Misra, Udayon. 2016. 'Victory for Identity Politics, Not Hindutva in Assam'. *Economic & Political Weekly* 51 (22): 20–23.

Mitra, Naresh. 2009. 'Minorities Cold to Congress'. *The Times of India*, 17 May.

Nath, Manoj. 2009. 'AUDF'. *Dainik Janambhumi*, 22 January.

Palshikar, Suhas, and Yogendra Yadav. 2009. 'Between Fortuna and Virtu: Explaining the Congress' Ambiguous Victory in 2009'. *Economic & Political Weekly* 44 (39): 33–46.

Palshikar, Suhas. 2017. *Indian Democracy*. New Delhi: Oxford University Press.

Prabhakara, M. S. 2012. *Looking Back into the Future Identity & Insurgency in Northeast India*. New Delhi: Routledge.

Priyadarshini, Susmita. 2011. 'Development Politics, Economic Welfare and AGP's Lost Game'. *The Assam Tribune*, 22 May.

Rahman, T. 2011. 'Pseudo Secularism in Politics'. *The Assam Tribune*, 24 March.

Saikia, Pahi. 2011. 'Assam Elections: Litmus Test for Democracy'. *The Assam Tribune*, 10 March.

Shastri, Sandeep, K. C. Suri, and Yogendra Yadav. 2009. *Electoral Politics in Indian States: Lok Sabha Elections in 2004 and Beyond*. New Delhi: Oxford University Press.

Talukdar, Sushant. 2009. 'Fractured Verdict'. *Frontline*, 5 June.

The Hindu. 2019. 'In Assam, Basic Dignity at Stake'. July 30.

The Times of India. 2015. 'Assam BJP Lauds Land Boundary Deal', 8 June.

The Times of India. 2018. 'There is a Genuine Issue of Illegal Immigration in Assam...Problem Is What Is to be Done Afterwards'. 10 September. Available at: https://timesofindia.indiatimes.com/blogs/talkingturkey/there-is-a-genuine-issue-of-illegal-immigration-in-assam-problem-is-what-is-to-be-done-afterwards/

Tripathi, Vikas, Tamasa Das, and Sandhya Goswami. 2018. 'National Narrative and Regional Subtext: Understanding the Rise of BJP in Assam'. *Studies in Indian Politics* 6 (1): 60–70.

Yadav, Yogendra, and Suhas Palshikar. 2008. 'Ten Theses on State Politics in India'. *Seminar* 591: 14–22.

ABOUT THE SERIES EDITORS AND AUTHOR

SERIES EDITORS

Rajeshwari Deshpande is a Professor of Politics at Savitribai Phule Pune University. She is a member of the editorial managing team of the journal *Studies in Indian Politics* and coordinates a forum on teaching and learning political science in India in the journal. She has published over 20 research articles in journals and has edited volumes in English as well as in Marathi. She has co-edited the book *Politics of Welfare: Comparisons across Indian States* (2015) with Louise Tillin and K. K. Kailash.

Suhas Palshikar taught Politics at Savitribai Phule Pune University and has been associated with Lokniti: Programme for Comparative Democracy of the Centre for the Study of Developing Societies. He is also the chief editor of the journal *Studies in Indian Politics*. He has co-edited two volumes on electoral politics: *Party Competition in Indian States: Electoral Politics in Post-Congress Polity* (2014) and *Electoral Politics in India: The Resurgence of the Bharatiya Janata Party* (2017). His most recent publication is *Indian Democracy: Meanings and Practices* (2017).

AUTHOR

Sandhya Goswami is former Professor in the Department of Political Science, Gauhati University, Guwahati, Assam. Currently, she is engaged with a rural-based NGO, SeSTA, working on social issues such as women's empowerment, literacy, livelihood and social justice. Her principal research interests include democracy, election studies and social movements.

She has authored *Language Politics in Assam* (1997), co-authored *North-East India Development, Communalism and Insurgency* (2007), and edited *Troubled Diversity: The Political Process in Northeast India* (2015). She has also published several research papers in prominent journals and edited books.

INDEX